ARM Assembly Language Programming With STM32 Microcontrollers

Learning By Example

By Yury Magda

To my wife, Julia

About the Author

Yury Magda is an embedded engineer experienced in designing hardware and software for Intel x86- and ARM-based systems. He is also the author of the books on designing embedded systems based upon various development platforms.

Contents

Introduction

This book offers a quick and easy way to learn low-level programming of
ARM microcontrollers using Assembly Language. The material of the book
aims at those who has some experience in programming and wants to learn
how to get more control over microcontroller hardware and improve overall
performance of embedded code.

Low-level programming comes into the category of more advanced
programming and involves some knowledge of a target microcontroller.
The material of this book is based upon the popular STM32 Cortex-M4
microcontrollers. It would be nice to have the datasheet, Programming and
Reference Manuals on the particular STM32 microcontroller on hand while
reading this book.

All examples are developed using the NUCLEO-L476RG development
board equipped with the STM32L476RGT6 Cortex microcontroller. The
program code is developed using a free STM32CubeIDE version 1.4.2.
The programming techniques described in this guide can also be applied to
other development boards equipped with Cortex-M4/L4 microcontrollers
(STM32F4xx, STM32F7, etc.) with corresponding changes in source code.
To develop the low-level code, the Assembler Language of
STM32CubeIDE was used. This assembly language supports a subset of the
ARM Thumb-2 instruction set that is a mix of 16- and 32-bit instructions
designed to be very efficient when using together with high-level languages.

Disclaimer

While the author has used good faith efforts to ensure that the information
and instructions contained in this book are accurate, the author disclaims all
responsibility for errors or omissions, including without limitation
responsibility for damages resulting from the use of or reliance on this
work. Use of the information and instructions contained in this work is at
your own risk. If any code samples or other technology this book contains
or describes is subject to open source licenses or the intellectual property
rights of others, it is your responsibility to ensure that your use thereof
complies with such licenses and/or rights. All example applications from
this book were developed and tested without damaging hardware. The
author will not accept any responsibility for damages of any kind due to
actions taken by you after reading this book.

Hardware and software

The material of this book covers programming the various types of ARM Cortex-M microcontrollers, therefore I used a few development boards with Cortex-M microcontrollers. Before you start learning embedded system with Cortex-M microcontrollers, you need some development tools. When we say "development tools", we assume both hardware and software. The "hardware" in this context means some development board equipped with a Cortex-M microcontroller, while the "software" means the development tool for writing, compiling, debugging and flashing the program code intended for a particular development board.

Selection of right hardware/software is a key point in learning embedded systems. Nowadays, the selection of software tools is even more important than selection of hardware, because this will determine your efforts and time required for learning embedded systems.

The material of this book is based upon using a popular low-cost NUCLEO-L476RG development board (**Fig.1**) that is described in detail on www.st.com.

Fig.1

The STM32 Nucleo boards don't require any separate probe as they integrate the ST-LINK/V2-1 debugger and programmer. These boards come with the STM32 comprehensive software HAL library together with various packaged software examples.

Important notes. All code examples represented in this book can easily be adapted to any STM32 development boards with Cortex-M4 – Cortex-M7 microcontrollers. If you use the boards with microcontrollers Cortex-M0, the part of capabilities such as low-level float-point operations will be unavailable, therefore for better experience I recommend you to take the board equipped at least with a Cortex-M4 microcontroller.

Once we have selected the development board for our experiments, we need to choose suitable software tools.

It is clear that you want to study ARM programming quickly. It is also clear that you want to get as much skills as possible during short time. Therefore, choosing the right software tools is extremely important.

Learning embedded programming will be fast and productive when we use a well-designed development tool that will be capable to do many things for you. The quality tool should be capable to do the following:

- generate the initializations code that puts core and peripherals in some predetermined state;
- write the code that configures a clocking system;
- enable clocking for desired peripheral devices;
- configure an interrupt system.

With such a development tool what is only needed is to implement your algorithm. All examples in this guide are developed using the powerful and free STM32CubeIDE development tool running in Windows 10. This tool provides graphical configuration tool from STMicro that simplifies configuration of the target device and generates C initialization code for the project. It relies on STM32Cube MCU Packages that contain device-specific descriptions, hardware abstraction layer (HAL) and a set of example applications.

The STM32CubeIDE tool must be installed on your PC before you begin to repeat the examples from this book.

Creating a template project in STM32CubeIDE

To learn Assembly Language coding, we will use the template project created by the STM32CubeMX Code Generator as is described below. Let's create a new STM32 Project in STM32CubeIDE by choosing **File → New → STM32 Project (Fig.2)**.

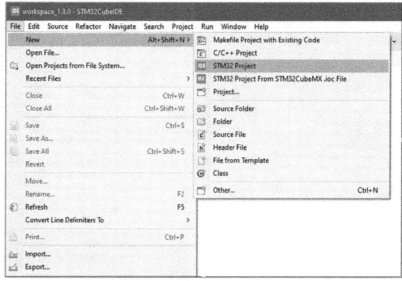

Fig.2

The Project Wizard will then start initializing the list of supported MCUs (**Fig.3**).

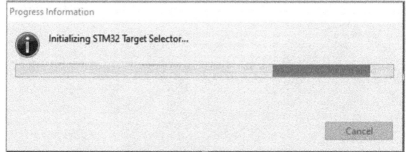

Fig.3

At this step, the list of supported MCUs and boards becomes visible. Since I use the NUCLEO-L476RG board with a Cortex-M4 microcontroller, I move to the **Board Selector** tab and select Nucleo-L476RG board (**Fig.4**).

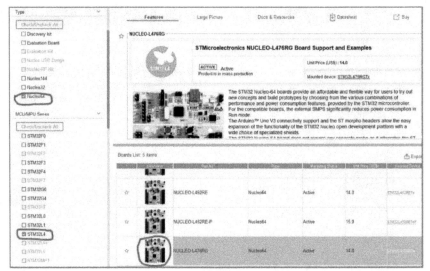

Fig.4

This is a place where you must select your MCU or board to work with. Clicking **Next** brings us to the next window where we should select the project name (**Fig.5**).

Fig.5

Let's assign the name **Project_1** to our project and click **Next**. The Project Wizard then sets up the firmware library package for the selected target (**Fig.6**).

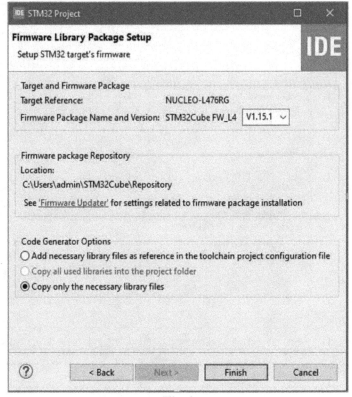

Fig.6

After clicking **Finish** the Project Wizard will install the corresponding firmware package if needed. You will also be prompted to initialize all peripherals with their default values (**Fig.7**).

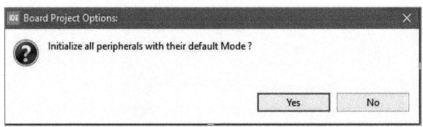

Fig.7

We can allow to do that by clicking **Yes**. When the following window (**Fig.8**) appears, simply click **Yes**.

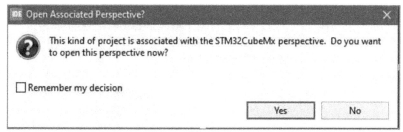

Fig.8

Next, we can configure the additional peripherals using the menu shown in the **Pinout view** window (**Fig.9**).

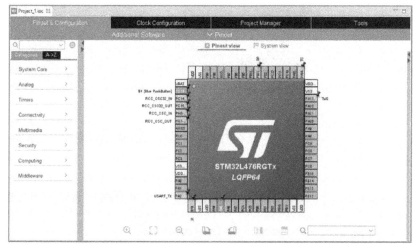

Fig.9

In this guide, the output of running demo applications will be transferred to an I/O console. For this purpose, I will add the new console using the USB-UART interface. For my NUCLEO-L476 board, this will be USART2 (**Fig.10**).

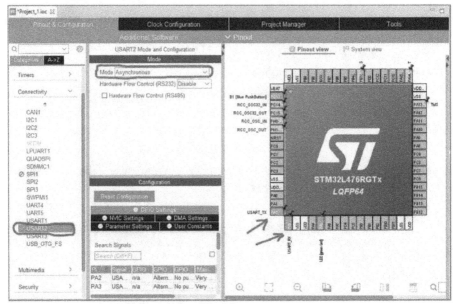

Fig.10

The parameters of USART2 are set on the **Parameter Settings** page (**Fig.11**).

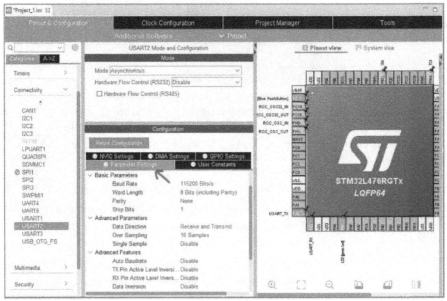

Fig.11

Note that USB-UART interface can be configured after a development board is connected to the USB port on the PC. In my case, USB-UART device appears in Windows 10 as follows (**Fig.12**).

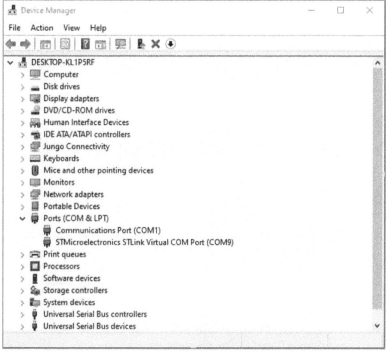

Fig.12

The parameters of the USB-UART device in **Device Manager** of Windows (**Fig.13**) must be the same as those set for an embedded UART (USART2, in my case).

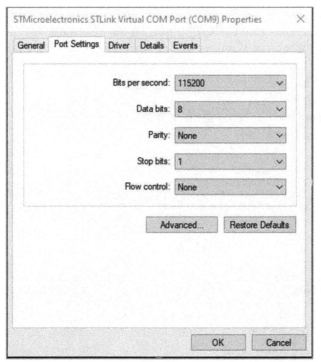

Fig.13

In this guide, I use the default parameters for USART2. **Note** that for your particular development board, the configuration of USB-UART may be different.

Finally, save the changes and allow the Project wizard to update the source code of a project.

Now I manually modify the source code of the **main()** function. To transfer data to the I/O console, I need some code that I will place into the stand-alone function named **disp_data()**.

At the beginning of **main()**, I placed a few lines (shown in bold, **Listing 1**).

Listing 1.

```
#include "main.h"
#include <stdio.h>
int cnt = 0;
```

Here, the **cnt** variable will be used to test the **disp_data()** function. Also the declaration of function **disp_data()** should be added to the main() source code (shown in bold, **Listing 2**).

Listing 2.

```
/* Private function prototypes --------------------*/

void SystemClock_Config(void);
static void MX_GPIO_Init(void);
static void MX_USART2_UART_Init(void);
void disp_data(int val);
```

The source code of **disp_data()** is shown in **Listing 3**.

Listing 3.

```
void disp_data(int val)
{
char buf[64];
int bRead;
bRead = sprintf(buf, "Returned: %d\n\r", val);
HAL_UART_Transmit(&huart2, (uint8_t*)buf, bRead, 300);
}
```

To test the **disp_data()** function, put the following code fragment (shown in bold) into the **while()** loop of a **main()** function as is shown in **Listing 4.**

Listing 4.

```
. . .
while (1)
{
disp_data(cnt++);
HAL_Delay(3000);
}
}
. . .
```

The modified source code of the **main()** function (most commented lines removed) will look like the following (**Listing 5**).

Listing 5.

```
#include "main.h"
```

```c
#include <stdio.h>
int cnt = 0;

/* Private function prototypes --------------------*/

void SystemClock_Config(void);
static void MX_GPIO_Init(void);
static void MX_USART2_UART_Init(void);
void disp_data(int val);

int main(void)
{

/* MCU Configuration---------------------------*/
/* Reset of all peripherals, Initializes the Flash interface and the SysTick. */

HAL_Init();

/* Configure the system clock */

SystemClock_Config();

/* Initialize all configured peripherals */

MX_GPIO_Init();
MX_USART2_UART_Init();

while (1)
{
disp_data(cnt++);
HAL_Delay(3000);
}
}
```

The running application will output the incremented value of the **cnt** variable to the I/O console every 3 s.

After the project is built, we can start debugging the code. First, configure the new I/O console in STM32CubeIDE to view the data transmitted through the USB-UART bridge.

On the right side of the **Console** window, select **Open Console** → **Command Shell Console (Fig.14)**.

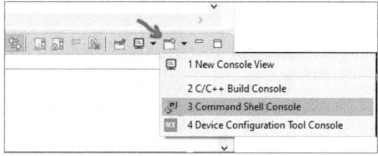

Fig.14

The **Select Remote Connection** window (**Fig.15**) appears.

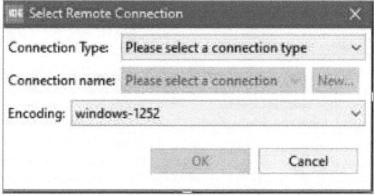

Fig.15

Then we should select the **Serial Port** as a connection type (**Fig.16**).

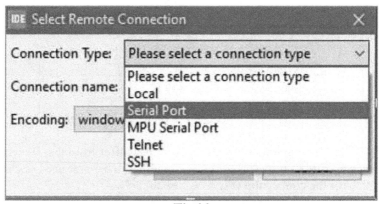

Fig.16

Then select **New…** (**Fig.17**).

Fig.17

This brings us to the next window (**Fig.18**) where we should set the parameters of the connection.

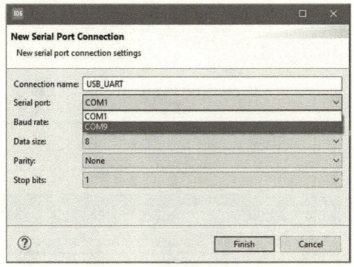

Fig.18

In my case, the ST Link USB-UART bridge appears as the serial port **COM9** that I name **USB_UART**.

Note that configuration for your board may differ from that shown above. Clicking **Finish** brings us to the next window, where we need to click **OK** to establish the connection (**Fig.19 – Fig.20**).

Fig.19

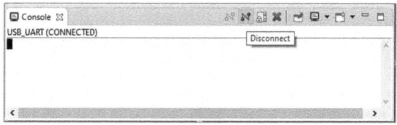

Fig.20

The running application produces the following console output (**Fig.21**).

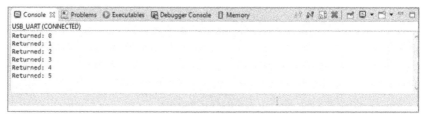

Fig.21

Now we have the code that does nothing but simply outputs data to the I/O console. To make this template project much more useful, we will add the source code written in Assembly Language. That will be done in the next sections.

Processing integers

This section contains the example codes for performing fast operations with integer numbers.

Before we begin, let's recall that the Assembly Language for Cortex-M microcontrollers (MCUs) operates with two types of registers, core and memory-mapped. The core MCU registers are used for data processing and controlling program flow, while the memory-mapped registers are used to control the peripheral devices such as digital input/output ports/pins (GPIO), timers, analog-to-digital converters, etc.

All MCU instruction use one or a few registers. Many MCU instructions require to indicate the register(s) explicitly, while other instructions use register(s) implicitly.

Example 1

This is one of the possible simplest examples of using assembly code. The **inv_int()** function whose source code is shown in **Listing 6** quickly reverses the sign of an integer number in the core register **r0** and returns the result in the same register. The function takes a single parameter in register **r0**.

Listing 6.

```
        .global inv_int
        .text
inv_int:
        neg   r0, r0
        bx    lr
```

Let's modify our template project **Project_1** in order to test the **inv_int()** function.

First, add the new file that will contain the source code from **Listing 6** to our project. To do that, move to the **Project Explorer**, then select **Core → Src → New → File (Fig.22)**.

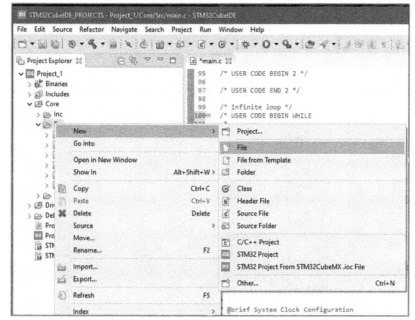

Fig.22

In the open window (**Fig.23**), name the assembly source file **inv_int.s** and click **Finish**. **Note** that this file must have **.s** extension.

Fig.23

Put the source code from **Listing 6** into **inv_int.s** (**Fig.24**) and save changes. Then we should make a few modifications of the source code in the **main()** function.

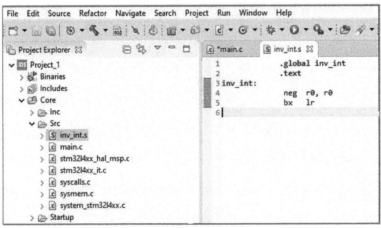

Fig.24

Then we should change the source code of the **main()** function by inserting a few lines of code (shown in bold, **Listing 7**).

Listing 7.

```
/* Includes ----------------------------------*/
#include "main.h"
#include <stdio.h>
#include <stdlib.h>
#include <time.h>

time_t t;
extern int inv_int(int i);
int num;

/* Private variables ----------------------------*/
UART_HandleTypeDef huart2;

/* Private function prototypes -----------------*/
void SystemClock_Config(void);
static void MX_GPIO_Init(void);
static void MX_USART2_UART_Init(void);
void disp_data(int val);

int main(void)
{

  /* Reset of all peripherals, Initializes the Flash
   * interface and the Systick. */
  HAL_Init();

  /* Configure the system clock */
  SystemClock_Config();

  /* Initialize all configured peripherals */
  MX_GPIO_Init();
  MX_USART2_UART_Init();

  /* Initializes random number generator */

  srand((unsigned) time(&t));
```

```
  while (1)
  {
   disp_data(inv_int(rand() % 50));
   HAL_Delay(3000);
  }
}

void disp_data(int val)
{
 char buf[128];
 int bRead;
 bRead = sprintf(buf, "Returned: %d\n\r", val);
 HAL_UART_Transmit(&huart2, (uint8_t*)buf, bRead, 300);
}
```

To use the function **inv_int()**, we should first declare it as **extern**:

extern int inv_int(int i);

The **inv_int()** function is then placed in the **while()** loop. The function takes a single parameter that is the random number generated by the library function **rand()**. The function inverts the sign of this number and returns the result to the **disp_data()** function. The loop repeats every 3 s.
The running application produces the following output to the I/O console (**Fig.25**).

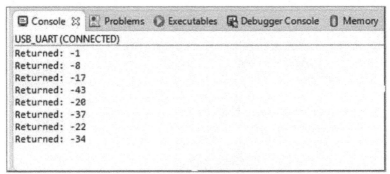

Fig.25

Example 2

This example illustrates operations with pointers to integer numbers. The following assembly code (function **inv_pint()**, **Listing 8**) quickly reverses

26

the sign of all elements in an integer array. The function takes 2 parameters in registers **r0** and **r1**. Register **r0** holds the address of the array and register **r1** holds the number of elements to be processed.

Listing 8.

```
            .global inv_pint
            .text
inv_pint:
            cmp     r1, #0
            ble     exit
next:
            ldr     r2, [r0]
            neg     r2, r2
            str     r2, [r0]
            sub     r1, r1, #1
            beq     exit
            add     r0, r0, #4
            b       next
exit:
            bx      lr
```

First what we need to do when the function is invoked is to check whether the array contains at least a single element. That is done by the instruction

cmp   r1, #0

Then all elements of the integer array are processed within a loop indicated by label **next**. In each iteration, the current element is first loaded into register **r2** by instruction

ldr   r2, [r0]

Then the sign of the element is reversed by the instruction

neg   r2, r2

Finally, the value in register **r2** is written back to the same address by the instruction

str   r2, [r0]

The instructions

sub   r1, r1, #1

27

```
beq    exit
```

check whether all elements of the array have been processed. If the unprocessed elements are available, the pointer to the array (register **r0**) is advanced by 4 by the instruction

```
add    r0, r0, #4
```

and the loop (label **next**) repeats.

To use the above function in our application, we need to save the source code from **Listing 8** in file **inv_pint.s** and add this file to the **\Core\Src** directory of our project.

Then we should insert a few lines of code (shown in bold) into the **main()** function as is shown in **Listing 9**.

Listing 9.

```
#include "main.h"
#include <stdio.h>

extern void inv_pint(int *num, int len);
int num[5] = {-57, -3, 11, 99, 2};

/* Private variables --------------------------*/
UART_HandleTypeDef huart2;

/* Private function prototypes ----------------*/
void SystemClock_Config(void);
static void MX_GPIO_Init(void);
static void MX_USART2_UART_Init(void);
void disp_data(int val);

int main(void)
{

  /* Reset of all peripherals, Initializes the Flash interface and the Systick. */
  HAL_Init();

  /* Configure the system clock */
  SystemClock_Config();
```

```c
/* Initialize all configured peripherals */
MX_GPIO_Init();
MX_USART2_UART_Init();

inv_pint(num, sizeof(num)/4);
for (int i = 0; i < sizeof(num)/4; i++)
{
  disp_data(num[i]);
}

while (1)
  {
  }
}

void disp_data(int val)
{
char buf[128];
int bRead;
bRead = sprintf(buf, "Returned: %d\n\r", val);
HAL_UART_Transmit(&huart2, (uint8_t*)buf, bRead,300);
}
```

Note that we can define the number of elements to be processed by the inv_pint() through its parameter **len**.

Example 3

Function **min_int()** whose assembly source code is shown in **Listing 10** searches for the minimum element in an integer array. The function takes 2 parameters, the address of the array (register **r0**) and the number of elements to be processed (register **r1**). The function returns the result in register **r0**.

Listing 10.

```
        .global    min_int
        .text
min_int:
        ldr    r2, [r0]
next:
        ldr    r3, [r0, #4]
```

```
        cmp   r2, r3
        ble   cont
        mov   r2, r3
cont:
        add   r0, r0, #4
        sub   r1, r1, #1
        cmp   r1, #1
        beq   exit
        b     next
exit:
        mov   r0, r2
        bx    lr
```

In this code, the current minimum is held in register **r2** that is initially loaded with the value of the first element of an array by the instruction

ldr r2, [r0]

Then all elements of the integer array are processed within a loop indicated by label **next**. In each iteration, the current element is loaded into register **r3** by the instruction

ldr r3, [r0, #4]

Then the current minimum (register **r2**) and the value in register **r3** are compared by the instruction

cmp r2, r3

The result of comparison is then used by the instruction

ble   cont

If the condition in the **cmp** instruction is false (**r2** > **r3**), the instruction

mov   r2, r3

will be executed. If the condition is true (**r2** ≤ **r3**), the **mov** instruction is skipped and control is passed to the instruction

add   r0, r0, #4

that advances the pointer (register **r0**) to the next element of the array. That is followed by the sequence

```
sub   r1, r1, #1
cmp   r1, #1
```

that allow to determine whether all elements have been processed.
If all elements are tested, the function returns the minimum element in
register **r0** and terminates. Otherwise, the loop (label **next**) repeats.

We should save the source code from **Listing 10** in file **min_int.s** and add
this file to the **\Core\Src** directory of our project.
To test **min_int()**, we should insert a few lines of code (shown in bold) into
the **main()** function (**Listing 11**).

Listing 11.

```
#include "main.h"
#include <stdio.h>

extern int min_int(int *num, int len);
int num[5] = {-57, 63, 11, -99, -542};

/* Private variables ----------------------------*/
UART_HandleTypeDef huart2;

/* Private function prototypes ------------------*/
void SystemClock_Config(void);
static void MX_GPIO_Init(void);
static void MX_USART2_UART_Init(void);
void disp_data(int val);

int main(void)
{
/* Reset of all peripherals, Initializes the Flash interface and the Systick. */
  HAL_Init();

/* Configure the system clock */
  SystemClock_Config();

/* Initialize all configured peripherals */
  MX_GPIO_Init();
  MX_USART2_UART_Init();

  disp_data(min_int(num, sizeof(num)/4));
```

31

```c
while (1)
{
}
}

void disp_data(int val)
{
char buf[128];
int bRead;
bRead = sprintf(buf, "Returned: %d\n\r", val);
HAL_UART_Transmit(&huart2, (uint8_t*)buf, bRead, 300);
}
```

It is easily to write the code searching the maximum element in an integer array. The assembly source code of the function (named **max_int()**) performing this task is shown in **Listing 12**.

Listing 12.

```
        .global    max_int
        .text
max_int:
        ldr    r2, [r0]
next:
        ldr    r3, [r0, #4]
        cmp    r2, r3
        bgt    cont
        mov    r2, r3
cont:
        add    r0, r0, #4
        sub    r1, r1, #1
        cmp    r1, #1
        beq    exit
        b      next
exit:
        mov    r0, r2
        bx     lr
```

Example 4

To compute the sum of the elements of an integer array the function **sum_ints()** whose assembly code is shown in **Listing 13** can be used. The function takes two parameters in the core registers **r0** and **r1**. Register **r0** contains the address of an integer array and **r1** contains the number of elements to be processed. The function returns the result in register **r0**.

Listing 13.

```
        .global    sum_ints
        .text
sum_ints:
        mov    r2, #0
next:
        ldr    r3, [r0]
        add    r2, r2, r3
        sub    r1, r1, #1
        cmp    r1, #0
        beq    exit
        add    r0, r0, #4
        b      next
exit:
        mov    r0, r2
        bx     lr
```

In this code, register **r2** holds the sum of elements of an array. Initially, register **r2** is cleared by instruction

mov r2, #0

The addition of elements is executed within the loop indicated by the label **next**. At the beginning of each iteration, the current element is loaded into register **r3** by instruction

ldr r3, [r0]

Next, the value in **r3** is added to the value in register **r2** by the instruction

add r2, r2, r3

Then the instruction

sub r1, r1, #1

decrements the loop counter in register **r1**. The next instruction

cmp r1, #0

33

checks if the loop counter = 0. If this condition is true, the loop exits by invoking the instruction

beq   exit

and the sum of elements is moved from register **r2** to **r0** by the instruction

mov   r0, r2

If the value in **r1** ≠ 0 (instruction cmp r1, #0), the pointer in register **r0** advances to the next element of the array by the instruction

add   r0, r0, #4

and the loop repeats.
We need to aave the source code from **Listing 13** in the file **sum_ints.s** and add this file to the **\Core\Src** directory of the project.
To test function **sum_ints()**, we must insert a few lines of code (shown in bold) into the **main()** function as is shown in **Listing 14**.

Listing 14.

```
#include "main.h"
#include <stdio.h>

extern int sum_ints(int *num, int len);
int num[5] = {-57, -63, -11, -99, -33};

/* Private variables -----------------------*/
UART_HandleTypeDef huart2;

/* Private function prototypes -------------*/
void SystemClock_Config(void);
static void MX_GPIO_Init(void);
static void MX_USART2_UART_Init(void);
void disp_data(int val);

int main(void)
{

  /* Reset of all peripherals, Initializes the Flash interface and the Systick. */
  HAL_Init();
```

```
/* Configure the system clock */
SystemClock_Config();

/* Initialize all configured peripherals */
MX_GPIO_Init();
MX_USART2_UART_Init();

disp_data(sum_ints(num, sizeof(num)/4));
while (1)
{
}
}

void disp_data(int val)
{
char buf[128];
int bRead;
bRead = sprintf(buf, "Returned: %d\n\r", val);
HAL_UART_Transmit(&huart2, (uint8_t*)buf, bRead, 300);
}
```

Example 5

Converting all integers of an array to positive values can be performed using the function **abs_val()** whose assembly source code is shown in **Listing 15**. The function **abs_val()** takes 2 parameters in the core register **r0** and **r1**. Register **r0** contains the address of the array and register **r1** contains the number of elements to be processed.

Listing 15.

```
        .global    abs_val
        .text
abs_val:
        ldr    r2, [r0]
        cmp    r2, #0
        bge    cont
        neg    r2, r2
        str    r2, [r0]
cont:
        sub    r1, r1, #1
        cmp    r1, #0
        beq    exit
```

```
        add   r0, r0, #4
        b     abs_val
exit:
        bx    lr
```

In this code, processing all elements of the array is performed within the loop indicated by the label **next**. At the beginning of each iteration, the current element is loaded into register **r2** by the instruction

ldr r2, [r0]

The value in **r2** is then compared with 0 by the instruction

cmp r2, #0

If the value in **r2** < 0, the sign of the value in **r2** is reversed and the result is stored at the same address in the array. These operations are performed by the sequence:

neg r2, r2
str r2, [r0]

The instruction

sub r1, r1, #1

decrements the loop counter in register **r1**. The instruction

cmp r1, #0

checks if the loop counter = 0. If this condition is true, the loop exits and the function terminates.

If the value in **r1** ≠ 0, the pointer in register **r0** advances to the next element of the array by the instruction

add r0, r0, #4

and the loop repeats.

To test the **abs_val()** function, the following lines of code (shown in bold) must be inserted into the **main()** function (**Listing 16**).

Listing 16.

```c
#include "main.h"
#include <stdio.h>

extern void abs_val(int *num, int len);
int num[6] = {-5, 0, 11, -90, -33, -1};

/* Private variables ----------------------------*/
UART_HandleTypeDef huart2;

/* Private function prototypes -------------------*/
void SystemClock_Config(void);
static void MX_GPIO_Init(void);
static void MX_USART2_UART_Init(void);
void disp_data(int val);

int main(void)
{

  /* Reset of all peripherals, Initializes the Flash interface and the Systick. */
  HAL_Init();

  /* Configure the system clock */
  SystemClock_Config();

  /* Initialize all configured peripherals */
  MX_GPIO_Init();
  MX_USART2_UART_Init();

  abs_val(num, sizeof(num)/4);
  for (int i = 0; i < sizeof(num)/4; i++)
  {
   disp_data(num[i]);
  }
  while (1)
  {
  }
}

void disp_data(int val)
{
 char buf[128];
 int bRead;
```

```
bRead = sprintf(buf, "Returned: %d\n\r", val);
HAL_UART_Transmit(&huart2, (uint8_t*)buf, bRead,300);
}
```

Example 6

This example illustrates how to optimize the loops while executing operations with arrays. We take the assembly source code from the previous example (function **abs_val()**, **Listing 15**) and rewrite it using the **cbz** MCU instruction. Using the **cbz** (or **cbnz**) instructions allows to avoid changing the condition code flags and to reduce the number of instructions.
This would especially be useful when processing the great number of elements in loops.
The modified code of function **abs_val()** is shown in **Listing 17**.

Listing 17.

```
          .global    abs_val
          .text
abs_val:
          ldr   r2, [r0]
          cmp   r2, #0
          bge   cont
          neg   r2, r2
          str   r2, [r0]
cont:
          sub   r1, r1, #1
          cbz   r1, exit
          add   r0, r0, #4
          b     abs_val
exit:
          bx    lr
```

In this code, the couple of instructions

cmp r1, #0
beq exit

is replaced with

cbz r1, exit

Example 7

This example illustrates multiplying integers with addition. The function **mul_add_ints()** whose source code is shown in **Listing 18** allows to multiply two integers and add some integer value to the result.
The function takes 4 parameters. Register **r0** contains the address of the first integer number to multiply, **r1** contains the address of a second number, **r2** contains the address of a destination where the result is saved. Register **r3** contains the number to be added.

Listing 18.

```
            .global    mul_add_ints
            .text
mul_add_ints:
            ldr    r0, [r0]
            ldr    r1, [r1]
            mla    r0, r0, r1, r3
            str    r0, [r2]
            bx     lr
```

To test the **mul_add_ints()** function, the following lines of code (shown in bold) must be inserted into the **main()** function (**Listing 19**).

Listing 19.

```
#include "main.h"
#include <stdio.h>

extern void mul_add_ints(int *a1,int *a2,int *dest, int num);
int a1[7] = {-2, 0, 1, -9, -33, -7, -9};
int a2[7] = {3, 6, 1, 3, -11, 5, -1};
int adest[7];

/* Private variables ----------------------------*/
UART_HandleTypeDef huart2;

/* Private function prototypes --------------------*/
void SystemClock_Config(void);
static void MX_GPIO_Init(void);
static void MX_USART2_UART_Init(void);
void disp_data(int val);
```

```c
int main(void)
{

/* Reset of all peripherals, Initializes the Flash interface and the Systick. */
HAL_Init();

/* Configure the system clock */
SystemClock_Config();

/* Initialize all configured peripherals */
MX_GPIO_Init();
MX_USART2_UART_Init();

for (int i = 0; i < sizeof(adest)/4; i++)
{
 mul_add_ints(&a1[i], &a2[i], &adest[i], 5);
 disp_data(adest[i]);
}
while (1)
{
}
}

void disp_data(int val)
{
char buf[128];
int bRead;
bRead = sprintf(buf, "Returned: %d\n\r", val);
HAL_UART_Transmit(&huart2, (uint8_t*)buf, bRead, 300);
}
```

The running application produces the following output (**Fig.26**).

```
Returned: -1
Returned: 5
Returned: 6
Returned: -22
Returned: 368
Returned: -30
Returned: 14
```

Fig.26

Example 8

This example is similar to the previous one except that multiplying integers is followed by subtraction. The function **mul_sub_ints()** whose assembly code is shown in **Listing 20** allows to multiply two integers and then subtract the result from some integer. The function takes 4 parameters. The core register **r0** contains the address of the first value to multiply, **r1** contains the address of a second value, **r2** contains the address of a destination where the result is saved. Register **r3** contains the value that is lessen by the result of multiplication.

Listing 20.

```
        .global    mul_sub_ints
        .text
mul_sub_ints:
        ldr    r0, [r0]
        ldr    r1, [r1]
        mls    r0, r0, r1, r3
        str    r0, [r2]
        bx     lr
```

To test **mul_sub_ints()**, we should insert the following lines of code (shown in bold) in the **main()** function as is shown in **Listing 21**.

Listing 21.

```
#include "main.h"
#include <stdio.h>

extern void mul_sub_ints(int *a1, int *a2, int *dest, int num);
int a1[7] = {-2, 0, 1, -9, -33, -7, -9};
int a2[7] = {3, 6, 1, 3, -11, 5, -1};
int adest[7];
```

/* Private variables --------------------------*/
UART_HandleTypeDef huart2;

/* Private function prototypes ----------------*/
void SystemClock_Config(void);
static void MX_GPIO_Init(void);

41

```c
static void MX_USART2_UART_Init(void);
void disp_data(int val);

int main(void)
{

    /* Reset of all peripherals, Initializes the Flash interface and the Systick. */
    HAL_Init();

    /* Configure the system clock */
    SystemClock_Config();

    /* Initialize all configured peripherals */
    MX_GPIO_Init();
    MX_USART2_UART_Init();

    for (int i = 0; i < sizeof(adest)/4; i++)
    {
     mul_sub_ints(&a1[i], &a2[i], &adest[i], 10);
     disp_data(adest[i]);
    }
    while (1)
    {
    }
}

void disp_data(int val)
{
 char buf[128];
 int bRead;
 bRead = sprintf(buf, "Returned: %d\n\r", val);
 HAL_UART_Transmit(&huart2, (uint8_t*)buf, bRead, 300);
}
```

The running application produces the following output (**Fig.27**).

```
USB_UART (CONNECTED)
Returned: 16
Returned: 10
Returned: 9
Returned: 37
Returned: -353
Returned: 45
Returned: 1
```

Fig.27

Example 9

This section shows how to write fast low-level code for arithmetic operations using the bit-shift MCU instructions. These instructions come in handy when we need to quickly multiply and divide integers.
A shift right effectively divides a number by 2 and a shift left multiplies it by 2. For example, the multiplication of two integers can be implemented as a combination of left-shifting operations and addition/subtraction.

The function **mul_4()** whose assembly code is shown in **Listing 22** illustrates quick multiplying an unsigned integer by 4. The function takes a single parameter (32-bit integer) in register **r0** and returns the result in the same register.

Listing 22.

```
        .global    mul4
        .text
mul4:
        lsl    r0, r0, #2
        bx     lr
```

To test **mul4()**, we need to insert a few lines of code (shown in bold) into the **main()** function (**Listing 23**).

Listing 23.

```
#include "main.h"
#include <stdio.h>
```

```c
extern int mul4(int a1);
int a1 = -11;

/* Private variables ----------------------------*/
UART_HandleTypeDef huart2;

/* Private function prototypes ------------------*/

void SystemClock_Config(void);
static void MX_GPIO_Init(void);
static void MX_USART2_UART_Init(void);
void disp_data(int val);

int main(void)
{

  /* Reset of all peripherals, Initializes the Flash interface and the Systick. */
  HAL_Init();

  /* Configure the system clock */
  SystemClock_Config();

  /* Initialize all configured peripherals */
  MX_GPIO_Init();
  MX_USART2_UART_Init();

  for (int i = 0; i < 4; i++)
  {
   a1 = mul4(a1);
   disp_data(a1);
  }
  while (1)
  {
  }
}

void disp_data(int val)
{
 char buf[128];
 int bRead;
 bRead = sprintf(buf, "Returned: %d\n\r", val);
 HAL_UART_Transmit(&huart2, (uint8_t*)buf, bRead, 300);
```

}

The running application produces the following output (**Fig.28**).

```
Returned:  -44
Returned:  -176
Returned:  -704
Returned:  -2816
```

Fig.28

Combining shift operations with addition and subtraction allows to implement fast multiplying by any integer number as is illustrated in the following source code examples.

Fast multiplying an unsigned integer by 5 may be implemented by the function **mul5()** whose assembly code is shown in **Listing 24**. The function takes a single parameter (32-bit unsigned integer) in register **r0**.

Listing 24.

```
        .global    mul5
        .text
mul5:
        mov    r1, r0
        lsl    r0, r0, #2
        add    r0, r0, r1
        bx     lr
```

In this code, the **lsl** instruction provides multiplying **r0** by 4. Then the **add** instruction adds the original value saved in register **r1** to **r0**, therefore register **r0** will contain the value that is 5 times the original one.

The following function (**mul15()**, **Listing 25**) provides fast multiplying the integer by 15. The function takes a single parameter (32-bit unsigned integer) in register **r0**.

Listing 25.

```
        .global    mul15
        .text
mul15:
        mov    r1, r0
```

```
lsl    r0, r0, #4
sub    r0, r0, r1
bx     lr
```

In this code, the original number in register **r0** is first shifted to the left by 4 (multiplied by 16). Then the value just obtained is reduced by subtracting the original value (16 − 1 = 15) held in register **r1**.

Processing floating-point numbers

STM32F4xx/STM32F7xx processors allow to perform operations with floating-point numbers due to availability of the floating point coprocessor (FPU).
The FPU fully supports single-precision add, subtract, multiply, divide, multiply, accumulate and square root operations. It also provides conversions between fixed-point and floating-point data formats, and floating-point constant instructions.
Note that the FPU is disabled from reset, therefore the program code should enable it before using. The initialization code of STM21CubeIDE enables FPU so we can immediately use it. Also, we should enable the float-point output by checking corresponding checkboxes in the
Project → Settings → MCU Settings → Tool Settings as is shown in **Fig.29**.

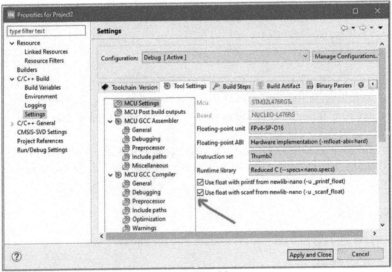

Fig.29

The FPU has 32 registers known as s0-s31 each of which can hold a single precision float. To transfer data between the FPU registers and the ARM core registers the **vmov** MCU instruction can be used.

Example 1

The function **max2f()** whose assembly code is shown in **Listing 26** searches for the maximum of two floating-point numbers. The function takes 2 parameters passed in the FPU registers **s0 – s1**. Register **s0** contains the first element to be compared, **s1** contains the second element. The function returns the result of operation in register **s0**.

Listing 26.

```
        .global max2f
        .text
max2f:
        vcmp.f32    s0, s1
        vmrs        APSR_nzcv, FPSCR
        bge         exit
        vmov.f32    s0, s1
exit:
        bx          lr
```

In this function, the numbers in registers **s0** and **s1** are compared by the instruction

vcmp.f32 s0, s1

This instruction sets the N, Z, C, and V flags in the Floating-Point Status Control Register (FPSCR). To analyze NZCV flags and make decision, it is needed to transfer the contents of FPSCR to the Application Program Status Register (APSR). The next instruction does that:

vmrs APSR_nzcv, FPSCR

If the value in the FPU register **s0** > **s1**, we need nothing to do. In this case, the instruction

bge exit

passes the control to the label **exit**.

If **s0** < **s1**, the value in register **s1** is moved into **s0**. In both cases, the result is returned in the FPU register **s0**.
The last instruction

```
bx  lr
```

passes control to the **main()** procedure.

To test the **max2f()** function, we should insert a few lines of code (shown in bold) into the **main()** function (**Listing 27**).

Listing 27.

```
#include "main.h"
#include <stdio.h>

extern float max2f(float f1, float f2);
float f1[10] = {67.09, -45.02, 2.35, -3.11, -11.5, 23.9, -95.2, -72.00, 11, 0.5};
float res;

/* Private variables ---------------------------*/
UART_HandleTypeDef huart2;

/* Private function prototypes --------------------*/
void SystemClock_Config(void);
static void MX_GPIO_Init(void);
static void MX_USART2_UART_Init(void);
void disp_fdata(float f1);

int main(void)
{
/* Reset of all peripherals, Initializes the Flash interface and the Systick. */
  HAL_Init();

  /* Configure the system clock */
  SystemClock_Config();

  /* Initialize all configured peripherals */
  MX_GPIO_Init();
  MX_USART2_UART_Init();

  res = max2f(f1[4], f1[9]);
  disp_fdata(res);
```

```
res = max2f(fl[0], fl[5]);
disp_fdata(res);
res = max2f(fl[7], fl[3]);
disp_fdata(res);

while (1)
{
}
}

void disp_fdata(float val)
{
char buf[128];
int bRead;
bRead = sprintf(buf, "Returned: %6.3f\n\r", val);
HAL_UART_Transmit(&huart2, (uint8_t*)buf, bRead, 300);
}
```

In this code, we introduce the code for the **disp_fdata()** that transmits the floating-point number to the I/O console.

The running application produces the following output (**Fig.30**).

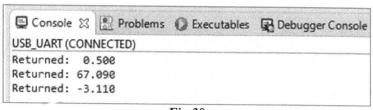

Fig.30

To find the minimum of 2 floating-point numbers, we can modify the source code for **max2f()** from **Listing 26**. The source code for our function named **min2f()** is shown in **Listing 28**.

Listing 28.

```
        .global min2f
        .text
min2f:
        vcmp.f32    s0, s1
        vmrs        APSR_nzcv, FPSCR
        blt         exit
        vmov.f32    s0, s1
exit:
```

```
        bx              lr
```

Example 2

Let's modify our pervious example so that we could operate with the addresses of numbers instead of their direct values.

The function **max2fp()** whose assembly code is shown in **Listing 29** searches for the maximum of two float numbers. The function takes 3 parameters passed in the core registers **r0** – **r2**. Register **r0** contains the address of a first element to be compared, **r1** contains the address of a second element and **r2** points to the buffer in memory where the result will be saved.

Listing 29.

```
        .global max2fp
        .text
max2fp:
        vldr.f32    s0, [r0]
        vldr.f32    s1, [r1]
        vcmp.f32    s0, s1
        vmrs        APSR_nzcv, FPSCR
        bge         set_s0
        vstr.f32    s1, [r2]
        b           exit
set_s0:
        vstr.f32    s0, [r2]
exit:
        bx          lr
```

In this code, both floating-point numbers are retrieved from the arrays pointed by registers **r0** and **r1** and placed in FPU registers **s0** and **s1** respectively. That is done by the sequence

vldr.f32 s0, [r0]
vldr.f32 s1, [r1]

Then the numbers in registers **s0** and **s1** are compared by the instruction

vcmp.f32 s0, s1

The above instruction when executed sets the N, Z, C, and V flags in the Floating-Point Status Control Register (FPSCR). To analyze NZCV flags and make decision, it is needed to transfer the contents of FPSCR to the Application Program Status Register (APSR). The next instruction does that:

```
vmrs      APSR_nzcv, FPSCR
```

Depending on the flags, the destination address in memory (core register **r2**) will contain the value either from **s0** or **s1**. That is implemented in the following sequence:

```
        bge        set_s0
        vstr.f32   s1, [r2]
        b          exit
set_s0:
        vstr.f32   s0, [r2]
```

To test the **max2fp()** function, we should insert a few lines of code (shown in bold) into the **main()** function (**Listing 30**).

Listing 30.

```
#include "main.h"
#include <stdio.h>

extern void max2fp(float *f1, float *f2, float *res);
float f1[7] = {-9.1, 40.8, -2.3,-1.5, 3.1,-5.2, 7.2};
float res;

/* Private variables ------------------------*/
UART_HandleTypeDef huart2;

/* Private function prototypes -----------------*/
void SystemClock_Config(void);
static void MX_GPIO_Init(void);
static void MX_USART2_UART_Init(void);
void disp_fdata(float f1);

int main(void)
{
/* Reset of all peripherals, Initializes the Flash interface and the Systick. */
  HAL_Init();
```

```
/* Configure the system clock */
SystemClock_Config();

/* Initialize all configured peripherals */
MX_GPIO_Init();
MX_USART2_UART_Init();

max2fp(&fl[0], &fl[6], &res);
disp_fdata(res);
max2fp(&fl[3], &fl[5], &res);
disp_fdata(res);
max2fp(&fl[2], &fl[4], &res);
disp_fdata(res);

while (1)
{
}
}

void disp_fdata(float val)
{
char buf[128];
int bRead;
bRead = sprintf(buf, "Returned: %6.3f\n\r", val);
HAL_UART_Transmit(&huart2, (uint8_t*)buf, bRead, 300);
}
```

The running application produces the following output (**Fig.31**).

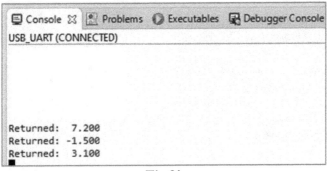

Fig.31

It is easily to modify the above code to search for the minimum of two floats (function **min2fp()**, **Listing 31**).

52

Listing 31.

```
        .global min2fp
        .text
min2fp:
        vldr.f32    s0, [r0]
        vldr.f32    s1, [r1]
        vcmp.f32    s0, s1
        vmrs        APSR_nzcv, FPSCR
        blt         set_s0
        vstr.f32    s1, [r2]
        b           exit
set_s0:
        vstr.f32    s0, [r2]
exit:
        bx          lr
```

To test the **min2fp()** function, we need to change the code of **main()** a bit. The modifications (in bold) are shown in **Listing 32**.

Listing 32.

```
#include "main.h"
#include <stdio.h>

extern void min2fp(float *f1, float *f2, float *res);
float f1[7] = {-9.1, 40.8, -2.3, -1.5, 3.1, -5.2, 7.2};
float res;

  . . .

min2fp(&f1[0], &f1[6], &res);
disp_fdata(res);
min2fp(&f1[3], &f1[5], &res);
disp_fdata(res);
min2fp(&f1[2], &f1[4], &res);
disp_fdata(res);

  . . .
```

The running application produces the following result (**Fig.32**).

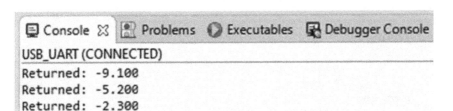

Fig.32

Example 3

The function **copy_posf()** whose assembly code is shown in **Listing 33** searches for all positive floating-point numbers in a source array and copies such numbers into a destination array. The function takes 3 parameters in the core registers **r0 – r2**. Register **r0** contains the address of the source array, register **r1** contains the address of the destination array and register **r2** contains the size of a source array. **Note** that the size of the destination array must be at least the same as that of the source array.

Listing 33.

```
            .global    copy_posfp
            .text
copy_posfp:
            cmp        r2, #0
            ble        exit
            vldr.f32   s0, [r0]
            vcmp.f32   s0, #0.0
            vmrs       APSR_nzcv, FPSCR
            bgt        write_num
            b          next
write_num:
            vstr.f32   s0, [r1]
next:
            add        r0, r0, #4
            add        r1, r1, #4
            sub        r2, r2, #1
            b          copy_posfp
exit:
            bx         lr
```

In this code, the first instruction

cmp   r2, #0

checks whether the number of elements to be copied is greater than 0 (**r2** > 0). If the condition is false (**r2** ≤ 0), the function immediately returns by invoking the instruction

```
ble   exit
```

If the condition is true (**r2** > 0), the current element in the source array is then checked by the sequence

```
vldr.f32    s0, [r0]
vcmp.f32    s0, #0.0
vmrs        APSR_nzcv, FPSCR
```

If this element is positive, it is copied into the destination array by the instruction

```
write_num:
            vstr.f32   s0, [r1]
```

The sequence beginning at the **next** label advances both source and destination pointers by 4, decreases the number of elements by 1 and branches to the next iteration:

```
next:
        add   r0, r0, #4
        add   r1, r1, #4
        sub   r2, r2, #1
        b     copy_posfp
```

When all elements have been processed (**r2** = 0), the function returns.

To test the function **copy_posfp()**, we should insert a few lines of code (shown in bold) into the **main()** function as is shown in **Listing 34**.

Listing 34.

```
#include "main.h"
#include <stdio.h>

extern void copy_posfp(float *src, float *dest, int len);
float fsrc[10] = {0.1, -4.8, -12.39, 1.99, 3.51, -10.2, 0.64, 22.7, -0.12, -3.08};
float fdest[10];
```

```
/* Private variables ---------------------------*/
UART_HandleTypeDef huart2;

/* Private function prototypes---------------*/
void SystemClock_Config(void);
static void MX_GPIO_Init(void);
static void MX_USART2_UART_Init(void);
void disp_fdata(float fl);

int main(void)
{
 /* Reset of all peripherals, Initializes the Flash interface and the Systick. */
 HAL_Init();

 /* Configure the system clock */
 SystemClock_Config();

 /* Initialize all configured peripherals */
 MX_GPIO_Init();
 MX_USART2_UART_Init();

 for (int i = 0; i < 10; i++)
 {
   fdest[i] = 0.0;
 }
   copy_posfp(fsrc, fdest, sizeof(fdest)/4);
   for (int i = 0; i < 10; i++)
   {
    disp_fdata(fdest[i]);
   }
  while (1)
  {
  }
 }

void disp_fdata(float val)
{
 char buf[128];
 int bRead;
 bRead = sprintf(buf, "Returned: %6.3f\n\r", val);
 HAL_UART_Transmit(&huart2, (uint8_t*)buf, bRead, 300);
}
```

The running application produces the following output (**Fig.33**).

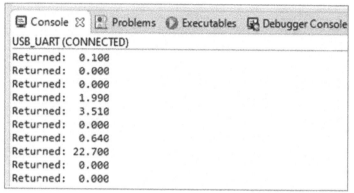

Fig.33

Example 4

The function **abs_fp()** whose assembly code is shown in **Listing 35** allows to convert each negative element of a source floating-point array into a positive value and write the result into a destination array. The function takes 3 parameters in registers **r0 – r2**. Register **r0** contains the address of the source array, register **r1** contains the address of the destination array and register **r2** contains the size of the source array. **Note** that the size of the destination array must be at least the same as that of the source array.

Listing 35.

```
          .global  abs_fp
          .text
abs_fp:
          cmp        r2, #0
          ble        exit
          vldr.f32   s0, [r0]
          vcmp.f32   s0, #0.0
          vmrs       APSR_nzcv, FPSCR
          blt        conv_num
          b          next
conv_num:
          vneg.f32   s0, s0
          vstr.f32   s0, [r1]
next:
          add        r0, r0, #4
```

```
        add       r1, r1, #4
        sub       r2, r2, #1
        b         abs_fp
exit:
        bx        lr
```

In this code, the instruction

```
cmp   r2, #0
```

checks whether the number of elements to be processed is equal to 0. If $r2 > 0$, the loop begins. When $r2 \leq 0$, the function immediately returns by invoking the instruction

```
ble   exit
```

Each current element in the source array is checked by the sequence

```
vldr.f32    s0, [r0]
vcmp.f32    s0, #0.0
vmrs        APSR_nzcv, FPSCR
```

If the element being checked is negative ($s0 < 0$), it is converted into a positive value and then copied into the destination array by the sequence:

```
conv_num:
            vneg.f32  s0, s0
            vstr.f32  s0, [r1]
```

The sequence beginning at the **next** label advances pointers in both source and destination arrays by 4, decreases the number of elements by 1 and branches to the next iteration (label **next**):

```
next:
      add   r0, r0, #4
      add   r1, r1, #4
      sub   r2, r2, #1
      b     abs_fp
```

When all elements have been processed ($r2 = 0$), the function returns.

To test the function **abs_fp()**, we should insert a few lines of code (shown in bold) into the **main()** function (**Listing 36**).

Listing 36.

```c
#include "main.h"
#include <stdio.h>

extern void abs_fp(float *src, float *dest, int len);
float fsrc[10] = {-0.1, 1.3, 13.39, -1.99, -0.51, 10.2, 0.64, -2.71, -0.12, 3.08};
float fdest[10];

/* Private variables -----------------------------------------------------*/
UART_HandleTypeDef huart2;

/* Private function prototypes -------------------------------------------*/
void SystemClock_Config(void);
static void MX_GPIO_Init(void);
static void MX_USART2_UART_Init(void);
void disp_fdata(float fl);

int main(void)
{

    /* Reset of all peripherals, Initializes the Flash interface and the Systick. */
    HAL_Init();

    /* Configure the system clock */
    SystemClock_Config();

    /* Initialize all configured peripherals */
    MX_GPIO_Init();
    MX_USART2_UART_Init();

    for (int i = 0; i < 10; i++)
    {
        fdest[i] = 0.0;
    }
    abs_fp(fsrc, fdest, sizeof(fdest)/4);
    for (int i = 0; i < 10; i++)
    {
     disp_fdata(fdest[i]);
    }
    while (1)
    {
    }
```

```
}
void disp_fdata(float val)
{
 char buf[128];
 int bRead;
 bRead = sprintf(buf, "Returned: %6.3f\n\r", val);
 HAL_UART_Transmit(&huart2, (uint8_t*)buf, bRead, 300);
}
```

The running application produces the following output (**Fig.34**).

Console ✕	Problems	Executables	Debugger Console

USB_UART (CONNECTED)
```
Returned:  0.100
Returned:  0.000
Returned:  0.000
Returned:  1.990
Returned:  0.510
Returned:  0.000
Returned:  0.000
Returned:  2.710
Returned:  0.120
Returned:  0.000
```

Fig.34

Example 5

With floating-point instructions, it is easy to write the fast code for complex operations. The function **mul_add_fp()** whose assembly code is shown in **Listing 37** illustrates how to implement multiplication and addition of elements of floating-point arrays.

The function takes 4 parameters in the core registers **r0 – r3**. Register **r0** contains the address of a first floating-point array, **r1** contains the address of a second array and **r2** contains the address of a third array.

Register **r3** contains the size of the destination array (this value should be the same for all arrays).

Each element of the first array addressed by **r0** will be moved into the FPU register **s0**, the elements of arrays addressed by **r1** and **r2** will be processed in the FPU registers **s1** and **s2** respectively.

The operation over **s0**, **s1** and **s2** is described by the following formula:

$$s2 = s0 * s1 + s2 \quad (1)$$

The result is stored in the FPU register **s2** addressed by the core register **r2**.

Listing 37.

```
            .global    mul_add_fp
            .text
mul_add_fp:
            cmp        r3, #0
            ble        exit
            vldr.f32   s0, [r0]
            vldr.f32   s1, [r1]
            vldr.f32   s2, [r2]
            vmla.f32   s2, s0, s1
            vstr.f32   s2, [r2]
            add        r0, r0, #4
            add        r1, r1, #4
            add        r2, r2, #4
            sub        r3, r3, #1
            b          mul_add_fp
exit:
            bx         lr
```

In this code, the number of elements to be processed is checked by the sequence

```
cmp   r3, #0
ble   exit
```

If **r3** > 0, the FPU registers **s0** – **s2** are loaded with the floating-point numbers from arrays by the sequence

```
vldr.f32   s0, [r0]
vldr.f32   s1, [r1]
vldr.f32   s2, [r2]
```

Then the instruction

```
vmla.f32   s2, s0, s1
```

performs the operation shown in the above formula (1) and the result is stored in the destination array using the instruction

```
vstr.f32   s2, [r2]
```

Then the following sequence

```
add      r0, r0, #4
add      r1, r1, #4
add      r2, r2, #4
sub      r3, r3, #1
b        mul_add_fp
```

advances the pointers to each array by 4, decrements the counter (register **r3**) by 1 and begins the next iteration.

To test the **mul_add_fp()** function, we need to insert a few lines of code (shown in bold) into the **main()** function (**Listing 38**).

Listing 38.

```
#include "main.h"
#include <stdio.h>

extern void mul_add_fp(float *src1, float *src2, float *dest, int len);
float fsrc1[3] = {7.1, -1.9, 3.5};
float fsrc2[3] = {3.3, -2.75, -8.11};
float fdest[3] = {1.5, 7.4, 2.2};

/* Private variables ---------------------------------------------------------*/
UART_HandleTypeDef huart2;

/* Private function prototypes -----------------------------------------------*/
void SystemClock_Config(void);
static void MX_GPIO_Init(void);
static void MX_USART2_UART_Init(void);
void disp_fdata(float fl);

int main(void)
{

  /* Reset of all peripherals, Initializes the Flash interface and the Systick. */
  HAL_Init();

  /* Configure the system clock */
  SystemClock_Config();

  /* Initialize all configured peripherals */
  MX_GPIO_Init();
  MX_USART2_UART_Init();
```

```
  mul_add_fp(fsrc1, fsrc2, fdest, sizeof(fdest)/4);
  for (int i = 0; i < 3; i++)
  {
   disp_fdata(fdest[i]);
  }
  while (1)
  {
  }
}

void disp_fdata(float val)
{
 char buf[128];
 int bRead;
 bRead = sprintf(buf, "Returned: %6.3f\n\r", val);
 HAL_UART_Transmit(&huart2, (uint8_t*)buf, bRead, 300);
}
```

The running application produces the following result (**Fig.35**).

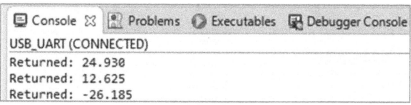

Fig.35

With the **vlms** MCU instruction it is easy to implement the following operation

$$s2 = s2 - (s0 * s1) \quad (2)$$

Below (**Listing 39**) is the source code of a **sub_mul_fp()** function that implements the operation from formula (2).

Listing 39.

```
            .global     sub_mul_fp
            .text
sub_mul_fp:
            cmp         r3, #0
            ble         exit
```

```
vldr.f32    s0, [r0]
vldr.f32    s1, [r1]
vldr.f32    s2, [r2]
vmls.f32    s2, s0, s1
vstr.f32    s2, [r2]
add         r0, r0, #4
add         r1, r1, #4
add         r2, r2, #4
sub         r3, r3, #1
b           sub_mul_fp
```
exit:
```
bx          lr
```

When using the floating-point arrays from **Listing 38**, the running application produces the following output (**Fig.36**).

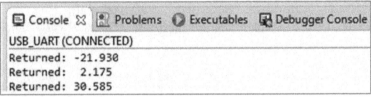

Fig.36

Example 6

When the embedded code operates with peripherals devices (GPIO, timers, analog-to-digital converters, etc.), the results are unsigned integers. Math processing such results needs that integers should be represented as floating-point numbers. There are a few useful instructions that helps us to do that.

The function **div_int_fp()** whose assembly code is shown in **Listing 40** illustrates how to divide two unsigned integers and get the floating-point result.

The function takes 4 parameters in the core registers **r0 – r3**. Register **r0** contains the address of a first array of unsigned integers, **r1** contains the address of a second array of unsigned integers, **r2** contains the address of a floating-point array where the results will be stored and register **r3** contains the number of elements to be processed.

Listing 40.

```
.global    div_int_fp
```

```
                    .text
div_int_fp:
            cmp              r3, #0
            ble              exit
            vldr.f32         s0, [r0]
            vcvt.f32.s32     s0, s0
            vldr.f32         s1, [r1]
            vcvt.f32.s32     s1, s1
            vcmp.f32         s1, #0.0
            vmrs             APSR_nzcv, FPSC
            bne              cont
            vstr.f32         s0, [r2]
            b                next
cont:
            vdiv.f32         s2, s0, s1
            vstr.f32         s2, [r2]
next:
            add              r0, r0, #4
            add              r1, r1, #4
            add              r2, r2, #4
            sub              r3, r3, #1
            b                div_int_fp
exit:
            bx               lr
```

In this code, the number of elements to be processed is checked by the sequence

```
cmp    r3, #0
ble    exit
```

If **r3** > 0, the FPU registers **s0 – s2** are loaded with the integers from both arrays, then these values are converted into the floating-point types by the sequence

```
vldr.f32       s0, [r0]
vcvt.f32.s32   s0, s0
vldr.f32       s1, [r1]
vcvt.f32.s32   s1, s1
```

Since we must not divide by 0.0, the following sequence checks whether the value in the FPU register **s1** ≠ 0.0:

```
vcmp.f32       s1, #0.0
vmrs           APSR_nzcv, FPSC
```

```
bne         cont
vstr.f32    s0, [r2]
```

In our case, if **s1** = 0.0, the code writes the value held in register **s0** into the destination address (register **r2**) and terminates the program.
If **s1** ≠ 0, the control is passed to the **cont** label and the following sequence will be executed:

```
cont:
        vdiv.f32   s2, s0, s1
        vstr.f32   s2, [r2]
```

In this sequence, the **vdiv** instruction divides the value in **s0** by **s1** and writes the result into register **s2**. The **vstr** instruction that follows writes the value in **s2** into the memory address pointed by register **r2**.
The sequence

```
add     r0, r0, #4
add     r1, r1, #4
add     r2, r2, #4
sub     r3, r3, #1
b       div_int_fp
```

advances the pointers to each array by 4, decrements the counter (register **r3**) by 1 and begins the next iteration.

To test the **div_int_fp()** function, we need to insert a few lines of code (shown in bold) into the **main()** function (**Listing 41**).

Listing 41.

```
#include "main.h"
#include <stdio.h>

extern void div_int_fp(int *src1, int *src2, float *dest, int len);
int src1[3] = {7, 9, 35};
int src2[3] = {12, 2, 6};
float fdest[3];

/* Private variables ---------------------------------------------------*/
UART_HandleTypeDef huart2;

/* Private function prototypes -----------------------------------------*/
```

```
void SystemClock_Config(void);
static void MX_GPIO_Init(void);
static void MX_USART2_UART_Init(void);
void disp_fdata(float fl);

int main(void)
{

    /* Reset of all peripherals, Initializes the Flash interface and the Systick. */
    HAL_Init();

    /* Configure the system clock */
    SystemClock_Config();

    /* Initialize all configured peripherals */
    MX_GPIO_Init();
    MX_USART2_UART_Init();

    div_int_fp(src1, src2, fdest, sizeof(fdest)/4);
    for (int i = 0; i < 3; i++)
    {
     disp_fdata(fdest[i]);
    }
    while (1)
    {
     }
}

void disp_fdata(float val)
{
 char buf[128];
 int bRead;
 bRead = sprintf(buf, "Returned: %6.3f\n\r", val);
 HAL_UART_Transmit(&huart2, (uint8_t*)buf, bRead, 300);
}
```

The running application produces the following output (**Fig.37**).

```
Console ⌗   Problems   Executables   Debugger Console
USB_UART (CONNECTED)
Returned:  0.583
Returned:  4.500
Returned:  5.833
```

67

Fig.37

Example 7

This is a bit complicated example of using floating-point MCU instructions. The function **reciprocal_sqrt()** whose assembly code is shown in **Listing 42** allows to compute the expression $1/\sqrt{x}$ for the elements of a floating-point array. This expression requires that **x** must always be > 0, therefore the operation will be performed only on the positive elements of the array. The function **reciprocal_sqrt()** takes 3 parameters in the core registers **r0** – **r2**. Register **r0** contains the address of a source array, register **r1** contains the address of a destination array and register **r2** contains the size of the source array. **Note** that the size of the destination array must be at least the same as that of the source array.

Listing 42.

```
                .global     reciprocal_sqrt
                .text
reciprocal_sqrt:
                cmp         r2, #0
                ble         exit
                vsub.f32    s4, s4, s4
                mov         r3, #1
next:
                vmov        s3, r3
                vcvt.f32.s32 s3, s3
                vldr.f32    s0, [r0]
                vcmp.f32    s0, s4
                vmrs        APSR_nzcv, FPSCR
                ble         cont
                vsqrt.f32   s0, s0
                vdiv.f32    s3, s3, s0
                vstr.f32    s3, [r1]
cont:
                sub         r2, r2, #1
                cmp         r2, #0
                beq         exit
                add         r0, r0, #4
                add         r1, r1, #4
                b           next
exit:
                bx          lr
```

In this code, we first check if the number of elements given by the third parameter (**r0**) is > 0 by the sequence:

```
cmp    r2, #0
ble    exit
```

Then we need to make two floating-point constants, 0.0 and 1.0. To make 0.0, we use the instruction:

```
vsub.f32    s4, s4, s4
```

The value = 0.0 will then be placed in the FPU register **s4**. The constant 1.0 that goes to the FPU register **s3** is made by the sequence

```
mov            r3, #1
vmov           s3, r3
vcvt.f32.s32   s3, s3
```

The operations on the elements of a source array are performed within a loop indicated by label **next**.
In each iteration, the code first checks if the current element loaded in register **s0** is > 0. This is done by the sequence:

```
vldr.f32    s0, [r0]
vcmp.f32    s0, s4
vmrs        APSR_nzcv, FPSCR
ble         cont
```

If **s0** ≤ 0, no operation is performed and control is passed to the **cont** label. The sequence

```
sub    r2, r2, #1
cmp    r2, #0
beq    exit
add    r0, r0, #4
add    r1, r1, #4
b      next
```

checks whether the end of the array is reached. If the condition is false, the code advances the pointers to the next elements in the array and the loop (label **next**) continues.

If the current element of the array (say, **x**) is positive, the following sequence computes the value $= 1/\sqrt{x}$ and writes the result into the destination array pointed by the core register **r1**:

```
vsqrt.f32    s0, s0
vdiv.f32     s3, s3, s0
vstr.f32     s3, [r1]
```

In this sequence, the instruction

```
vsqrt.f32    s0, s0
```

computes the square root of the value in the FPU register **s0** and writes the result back into the same register. Thus, when this instruction succeeds, we get the value $= \sqrt{x}$ in **s0**.
The following instruction in this section computes the value $= 1/\sqrt{x}$ and stores the result in the FPU register **s3**:

```
vdiv.f32    s3, s3, s0
```

When this instruction succeeds, the value $= 1/\sqrt{x}$ is stored in the FPU register **s3**. Finally, the value in **s3** is written into the array at the address pointed by register **r1**. That is done by instruction

```
vstr.f32    s3, [r1]
```

To test the **reciprocal_sqrt()** function, we should insert a few lines of code (shown in bold) into the **main()** function (**Listing 43**).

Listing 43.

```
#include "main.h"
#include <stdio.h>

extern void reciprocal_sqrt(float *src, float *dest, int len);
float src[10] = {1.55, 0.0, -17.8, 99.99, -3.5, 2.0, 0.33, 12.9, 0.0, 11.0};
float dest[10] = {0.0, 0.0, 0.0, 0.0, 0.0, 0.0, 0.0, 0.0, 0.0, 0.0};

/* Private variables ------------------------------------------------------*/
UART_HandleTypeDef huart2;

/* Private function prototypes --------------------------------------------*/
void SystemClock_Config(void);
```

```c
static void MX_GPIO_Init(void);
static void MX_USART2_UART_Init(void);
void disp_fdata(float f1);

int main(void)
{

  /* Reset of all peripherals, Initializes the Flash interface and the Systick. */
  HAL_Init();

   /* Configure the system clock */
  SystemClock_Config();

  /* Initialize all configured peripherals */
  MX_GPIO_Init();
  MX_USART2_UART_Init();

  reciprocal_sqrt(src, dest, sizeof(src)/4);
  for (int i = 0; i < 10; i++)
  {
   disp_fdata(dest[i]);
  }

  while (1)
  {
  }
}

void disp_fdata(float val)
{
 char buf[128];
 int bRead;
 bRead = sprintf(buf, "Returned: %6.3f\n\r", val);
 HAL_UART_Transmit(&huart2, (uint8_t*)buf, bRead, 300);
}
```

The running application produces the following output (**Fig.38**).

```
Console 🔀  Problems  ▶ Executables  🔧 Debugger Console
USB_UART (CONNECTED)
Returned:  0.803
Returned:  0.000
Returned:  0.000
Returned:  0.100
Returned:  0.000
Returned:  0.707
Returned:  1.741
Returned:  0.278
Returned:  0.000
Returned:  0.302
```

Fig.38

Example 8

In this example, the function **mean_fp()** whose assembly language source code is shown in **Listing 44** computes the **Mean** (denoted μ) of a numbers kept in the floating-point array.
The formula for calculating the Mean is given below:

$$\mu = (x_1 + x_2 + x_3 + \ldots + x_N) / N \quad (1),$$

where **N** is the number of elements of the array $x_1 \ldots x_N$.

The function takes 3 parameters in the core registers **r0 – r2**. Register **r0** contains the address of the source floating-point array, register **r1** contains the address of a destination floating-point number and **r2** specifies the size of the source array.

Listing 44.

```
        .global    mean_fp
        .text
mean_fp:
        cmp            r2, #0
        ble            exit
        vsub.f32       s2, s2, s2
        vmov           s1, r2
        vcvt.f32.s32   s1, s1
next:
        vldr.f32       s0, [r0]
        vadd.f32       s2, s2, s0
        sub            r2, r2, #1
```

72

```
            cmp        r2, #0
            beq        cont
            add        r0, r0, #4
            b          next
cont:
            vdiv.f32   s2, s2, s1
            vstr.f32   s2, [r1]
exit:
            bx         lr
```

In this code, the sequence

```
cmp    r2, #0
ble    exit
```

checks whether the number of elements to be processed is > 0. If this condition is true, the following instruction

```
vsub.f32    s2, s2, s2
```

moves 0 to the FPU register **s2** – this register will contain the sum of elements.
The next two instructions

```
vmov        s1, r2
vcvt.f32.s32  s1, s1
```

creates the floating-point constant **N** (see formula (1)) from integer held in register **r2**. The floating-point **N** is then put into the FPU register **s1**.
The addition of the elements of the array is implemented by the sequence

```
vldr.f32    s0, [r0]
vadd.f32    s2, s2, s0
```

The next fragment of code

```
sub    r2, r2, #1
cmp    r2, #0
beq    cont
add    r0, r0, #4
b      next
```

first checks whether all elements in the array are processed. If the end of the array is not reached (**r2** > 0), the pointer in register **r0** advances by 4 and the loop (label **next**) repeats.

When loop exits (label **cont**), the FPU register **s0** will contain the sum of the elements. Then the code divides this sum by the number of elements using the instruction

vdiv.f32   s2, s2, s1

Finally, the result is written into the destination address held in register **r1** by the instruction

vstr.f32   s2, [r1]

To test the function **mean_fp()**, we should insert a few lines of code (shown in bold) into the **main()** function (**Listing 45**).

Listing 45.

```
#include "main.h"
#include <stdio.h>

extern void mean_fp(float *src, float *dest, int len);
float src[6] = {1.55, 0.0, 17.8, 9.99, 3.5, 2.0};
float dest;

/* Private variables ----------------------------------------------------------*/
UART_HandleTypeDef huart2;

/* Private function prototypes -------------------------------------------------*/
void SystemClock_Config(void);
static void MX_GPIO_Init(void);
static void MX_USART2_UART_Init(void);
void disp_fdata(float f1);

int main(void)
{

/* Reset of all peripherals, Initializes the Flash interface and the Systick. */
  HAL_Init();

/* Configure the system clock */
  SystemClock_Config();
```

```
/* Initialize all configured peripherals */
MX_GPIO_Init();
MX_USART2_UART_Init();

mean_fp(src, &dest, sizeof(src)/4);
disp_fdata(dest);

while (1)
{
}
}

void disp_fdata(float val)
{
char buf[128];
int bRead;
bRead = sprintf(buf, "Returned: %6.3f\n\r", val);
HAL_UART_Transmit(&huart2, (uint8_t*)buf, bRead, 300);
}
```

The running application produces the following output (**Fig.39**).

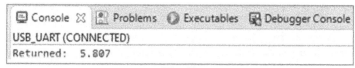

Fig.39

Example 9

This is a modified version of the previous example. Here the function **mean_fp()** returns the result to the **main()** as a floating-point value. This function takes only 2 parameters in the core registers **r0** and **r1** and returns the result in the FPU register **s0**.
The modified source code of **mean_fp()** is given in **Listing 46**.

Listing 46.

```
        .global    mean_fp
        .text
mean_fp:
```

```
           cmp              r1, #0
           ble              exit
           vsub.f32         s2, s2, s2
           vmov             s1, r1
           vcvt.f32.s32     s1, s1
next:
           vldr.f32         s0, [r0]
           vadd.f32         s2, s2, s0
           sub              r1, r1, #1
           cmp              r1, #0
           beq              cont
           add              r0, r0, #4
           b                next
cont:
           vdiv.f32         s2, s2, s1
           vmov.f32         s0, s2
exit:
           bx               lr
```

To test the function **mean_fp()**, we need to insert a few lines of code (shown in bold) into the **main()** function **(Listing 47)**.

Listing 47.

```
#include "main.h"
#include <stdio.h>

extern float mean_fp(float *src, int len);
float src[6] = {-8.33, 1.0, 27.07, 0.99, -3.9, 0.0};
float dest;

/* Private variables -------------------------------------------------*/
UART_HandleTypeDef huart2;

/* Private function prototypes ---------------------------------------*/
void SystemClock_Config(void);
static void MX_GPIO_Init(void);
static void MX_USART2_UART_Init(void);
void disp_fdata(float f1);

int main(void)
{

   /* Reset of all peripherals, Initializes the Flash interface and the Systick. */
   HAL_Init();
```

```
/* Configure the system clock */
SystemClock_Config();

/* Initialize all configured peripherals */
MX_GPIO_Init();
MX_USART2_UART_Init();

disp_fdata(mean_fp(src, sizeof(src)/4));

while (1)
{
}
}

void disp_fdata(float val)
{
char buf[128];
int bRead;
bRead = sprintf(buf, "Returned: %6.3f\n\r", val);
HAL_UART_Transmit(&huart2, (uint8_t*)buf, bRead, 300);
}
```

The running application produces the following output (**Fig.40**).

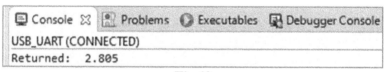

Fig.40

Example 10

In this example, we will compute the **Root Mean Square** (RMS) of the set of floating-point numbers using the formula

$$\text{RMS} = \sqrt{(x_1^2 + x_2^2 + \ldots x_N^2)/N} \quad (1),$$

where $x_1, x_2, \ldots, x_N$ – elements of floating-point array containing N numbers.

This operation will be implemented using the function **rms_fp()** whose assembly source code is shown in **Listing 48**. The function takes 2 parameters in the core registers **r0 – r1**. Register **r0** contains the address of a source floating-point array, register **r1** contains the address of a destination floating-point number. The function returns the floating-point value in the FPU register **s0**.

Listing 48.

```
        .global     rms_fp
        .text
rms_fp:
        cmp             r1, #0
        ble             exit
        vsub.f32        s2, s2, s2
        vmov            s1, r1
        vcvt.f32.s32    s1, s1
next:
        vldr.f32        s0, [r0]
        vmul.f32        s0, s0, s0
        vadd.f32        s2, s2, s0
        sub             r1, r1, #1
        cmp             r1, #0
        beq             cont
        add             r0, r0, #4
        b               next
cont:
        vdiv.f32        s2, s2, s1
        vsqrt.f32       s2, s2
        vmov.f32        s0, s2
exit:
        bx              lr
```

In this code, the sequence

```
cmp   r1, #0
ble   exit
```

checks whether the number of elements to be processed is > 0. If this condition is true, the instruction

```
vsub.f32   s2, s2, s2
```

moves 0 to the FPU register **s2** – this register will contain the sum of elements.

The next two instructions

```
vmov          s1, r1
vcvt.f32.s32  s1, s1
```

put the floating-point constant **N** (see formula (1)) in the FPU register **s1**. In our example, the integer number **N** is initially held in register **r1**. The following MCU instructions

```
vldr.f32   s0, [r0]
vmul.f32   s0, s0, s0
vadd.f32   s2, s2, s0
```

within the loop (label **next**) execute the calculation of the sum

$$x_1^2 + x_2^2 + \ldots x_N^2$$

The next sequence

```
sub   r1, r1, #1
cmp   r1, #0
beq   cont
add   r0, r0, #4
b     next
```

first checks if all elements in the array are processed. If the end of the array is not reached (**r1** > 0), the pointer in register **r0** advances by 4 and the loop (label **next**) repeats.

When loop exits (label **cont**), the FPU register **s0** will contains the sum of the elements. Then the code calculates RMS using the following sequence:

```
vdiv.f32   s2, s2, s1
vsqrt.f32  s2, s2
```

The result is finally copied from the FPU register **s2** into **s0** by the instruction:

```
vmov.f32   s0, s2
```

To test the **rms_fp()** function, we should insert a few lines of code (shown in bold) into the main() function (**Listing 49**).

Listing 49.

```c
#include "main.h"
#include <stdio.h>

extern float rms_fp(float *src, int len);
float src[6] = {1.33, 1.9, 7.05, 0.99, 3.9, 0.5};
float dest;

/* Private variables ---------------------------------------------------*/
UART_HandleTypeDef huart2;

/* Private function prototypes ------------------------------------------*/
void SystemClock_Config(void);
static void MX_GPIO_Init(void);
static void MX_USART2_UART_Init(void);
void disp_fdata(float fl);

int main(void)
{

  /* Reset of all peripherals, Initializes the Flash interface and the Systick. */
  HAL_Init();

  /* Configure the system clock */
  SystemClock_Config();

  /* Initialize all configured peripherals */
  MX_GPIO_Init();
  MX_USART2_UART_Init();

  disp_fdata(rms_fp(src, sizeof(src)/4));

  while (1)
  {
  }
}

void disp_fdata(float val)
{
 char buf[128];
 int bRead;
 bRead = sprintf(buf, "Returned: %6.3f\n\r", val);
 HAL_UART_Transmit(&huart2, (uint8_t*)buf, bRead, 300);
```

}

The running application produces the following output (**Fig.41**).

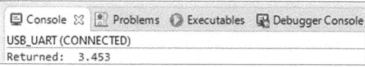

Fig.41

Bit and byte operations

This section illustrates using the Cortex-M instructions operating with bits and bytes of a 32-bit word.

Example 1

The function **clear_bit()** whose source code is shown in **Listing 50** allows to clear any bit of 32-bit unsigned integer. The function takes 2 parameters in registers **r0** and **r1**. Register **r0** contains the 32-bit value and **r1** specifies the position of a bit to be cleared.

Listing 50.

```
        .global    clear_bit
        .text
clear_bit:
        mov     r2, #1
        lsl     r2, r1
        bic     r0, r2
        bx      lr
```

In this code, the **bic** MCU instruction is used to clear a target bit. We need to save the above code in the file **clear_bit.s** and add this file to the **\Core\Src** directory of our project.
To test the **clear_bit()** function, we should insert a few lines of code (shown in bold) into the **main()** function (**Listing 51**).

Listing 51.

#include "main.h"

```c
extern uint32_t clear_bit(uint32_t num, uint32_t pos);
uint32_t num = 1379;
uint32_t pos = 6;
uint32_t res;

/* Private variables --------------------------------------------------------*/
UART_HandleTypeDef huart2;

/* Private function prototypes ----------------------------------------------*/
void SystemClock_Config(void);
static void MX_GPIO_Init(void);
static void MX_USART2_UART_Init(void);

int main(void)
{

  /* Reset of all peripherals, Initializes the Flash interface and the Systick. */
  HAL_Init();

  /* Configure the system clock */
  SystemClock_Config();

  /* Initialize all configured peripherals */
  MX_GPIO_Init();
  MX_USART2_UART_Init();

  res = clear_bit(num, pos);
  while (1)
  {
  }
}
```

In this code, the function **clear_bit()** clears bit 6 in variable **num** (=1379). The variable **res** will then be assigned the value = 1315.

After the project has been built, we can start debugging. To view the result of operation, we should add two variables, **num** and **pos**, in the **Expressions** window. To do that, select **Window → Show View → Expressions (Fig.42)**.

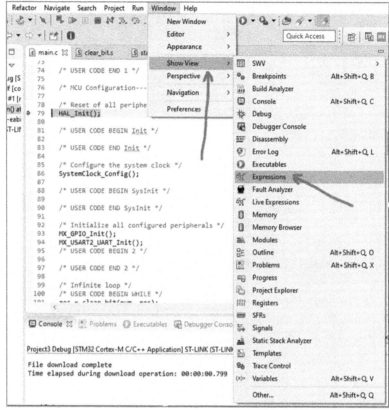

Fig.42

The following page (**Fig.43**) opens. Here we need to add 3 variables, **num**, **pos** and **res** (**Fig.44**).

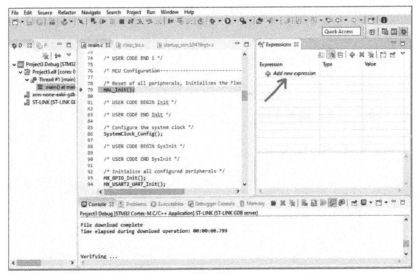

Fig.43

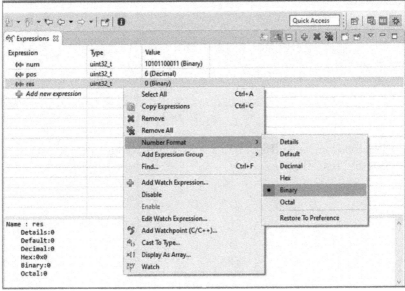

Fig.44

To observe the values in binary format, we also need to explicitly select this option by right-clicking on the corresponding field (see **Fig.44**).
When we are done, we can continue debugging. After the function **clear_bit()** terminates, we will see the result of operation (**Fig.45**).

Fig.45

Example 2

Setting the bit of a 32-bit unsigned integer can be performed by function **set_bit()** whose code is shown below (**Listing 52**). The function takes 2 parameters in the core registers **r0** and **r1**. Register **r0** contains the 32-bit value and **r1** specifies the position of a bit to be set.

Listing 52.

```
        .global    set_bit
        .text
set_bit:
        mov    r2, #1
        lsl    r2, r1
        orr    r0, r2
        bx     lr
```

In this code, we use the **orr** MCU instruction to set a target bit. It is easily to test this function using the **main()** function from the previous example (**Listing 51**). To do that, we only need to replace the definitions of **clear_bit()** with **set_bit()**.
The result of operation is shown in **Fig.46**.

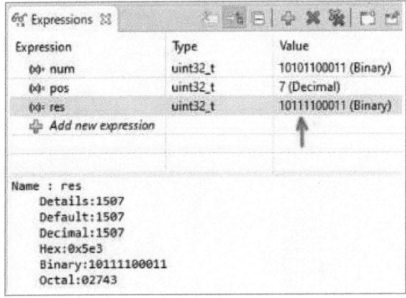

Fig.46

Example 3

Toggling the bit of a 32-bit unsigned integer can be performed by function **toggle_bit()** whose code is shown below (**Listing 53**). The function takes 2 parameters in registers **r0** and **r1**. Register **r0** contains the 32-bit number and **r1** specifies the position of a bit to be toggled.

Listing 53.

```
        .global   toggle_bit
        .text
toggle_bit:
        mov   r2, #1
        lsl   r2, r1
        eor   r0, r2
```

```
bx    lr
```

In this code, we use the **eor** MCU instruction to toggle a target bit.

To test the **toggle_bit()** function, we can insert a few lines of code (shown in bold) into the **main()** function (**Listing 54**).

Listing 54.

```
#include "main.h"
extern uint32_t toggle_bit(uint32_t num, uint32_t pos);
uint32_t num = 1379;
uint32_t pos = 7;
uint32_t res;

/* Private variables -----------------------------------------------*/
UART_HandleTypeDef huart2;

/* Private function prototypes -------------------------------------*/
void SystemClock_Config(void);
static void MX_GPIO_Init(void);
static void MX_USART2_UART_Init(void);

int main(void)
{
/* Reset of all peripherals, Initializes the Flash interface and the Systick. */
  HAL_Init();

/* Configure the system clock */
  SystemClock_Config();

/* Initialize all configured peripherals */
  MX_GPIO_Init();
  MX_USART2_UART_Init();

  while (1)
  {
    res = toggle_bit(num, pos);
    num = res;
    HAL_Delay(1000);
  }
}
```

The result of operation can be viewed in the **Expressions** window.

Example 4

The function **clear_bf()** whose assembly source code is shown in **Listing 55** provides fast clearing the bitfield of a 32-bit unsigned integer. The function takes 3 parameters in the core registers **r0 – r2**. Register **r0** contains the 32-bit value, **r1** specifies the position of the least significant bit of a bitfield and **r2** specifies the width of the bitfield.

Listing 55.

```
        .global    clear_bf
        .text
clear_bf:
        cmp   r1, #0
        blt   exit
        cmp   r2, #0
        ble   exit
        mov   r3, #1
        lsl   r3, r2
        sub   r3, r3, #1
        lsl   r3, r1
        mvn   r3, r3
        and   r0, r0, r3
exit:
        bx    lr
```

To test the **clear_bf()** function, we need to insert the a few lines of code (shown in bold) into the **main()** function (**Listing 56**).

Listing 56.

```
#include "main.h"
extern uint32_t clear_bf(uint32_t num, uint32_t pos, uint32_t width);

uint32_t num = 0;
uint32_t pos = 0;
uint32_t width = 9;
uint32_t res;

/* Private variables ---------------------------------------------------*/
UART_HandleTypeDef huart2;
```

```c
/* Private function prototypes ---------------------------------------*/
void SystemClock_Config(void);
static void MX_GPIO_Init(void);
static void MX_USART2_UART_Init(void);

int main(void)
{

  /* Reset of all peripherals, Initializes the Flash interface and the Systick. */
  HAL_Init();

  /* Configure the system clock */
  SystemClock_Config();

  /* Initialize all configured peripherals */
  MX_GPIO_Init();
  MX_USART2_UART_Init();

  res = clear_bf(num, pos, width);
  while (1)
  {
  }
}
```

The result of operation for the parameters

```c
uint32_t num = 16383;
uint32_t pos = 0;
uint32_t width = 9;
```

is shown in **Fig.47**.

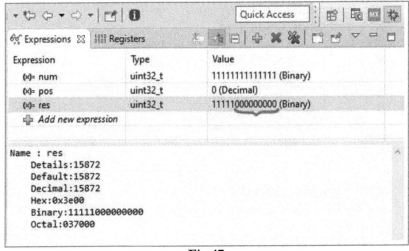

Fig.47

The result of operation for the parameters

uint32_t num = 16383;
uint32_t pos = 7;
uint32_t width = 3;

is shown in **Fig.48**.

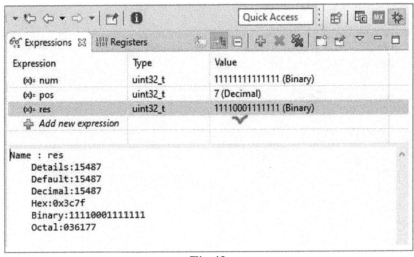

Fig.48

Example 5

The function **set_bf()**) whose assembly source code is shown in **Listing 57** provides fast setting the bitfield of a 32-bit unsigned integer. The function takes 3 parameters in registers **r0 – r2**. Register **r0** contains the 32-bit value, **r1** specifies the position of the least significant bit of the bitfield and **r2** specifies the width of the bitfield.

Listing 57.

```
        .global   set_bf
        .text
set_bf:
        cmp    r1, #0
        blt    exit
        cmp    r2, #0
        ble    exit
        mov    r3, #1
        lsl    r3, r2
        sub    r3, r3, #1
        lsl    r3, r1
        orr    r0, r0, r3
exit:
        bx     lr
```

To test the **set_bf()** function, we need to insert a few lines of code (shown in bold) into the **main()** function (**Listing 58**).

Listing 58.

```
#include "main.h"
extern uint32_t set_bf(uint32_t num, uint32_t pos, uint32_t width);

uint32_t num = 0;
uint32_t pos = 5;
uint32_t width = 3;
uint32_t res;
```

/* Private variables --*/
UART_HandleTypeDef huart2;

/* Private function prototypes --*/
void SystemClock_Config(void);
static void MX_GPIO_Init(void);

```
static void MX_USART2_UART_Init(void);

int main(void)
{

  /* Reset of all peripherals, Initializes the Flash interface and the Systick. */
  HAL_Init();

  /* Configure the system clock */
  SystemClock_Config();

  /* Initialize all configured peripherals */
  MX_GPIO_Init();
  MX_USART2_UART_Init();

  res = set_bf(num, pos, width);

  while (1)
  {
  }
}
```

For the given parameters of function **set_bf()**, the result of operation will look like the following (**Fig.49**).

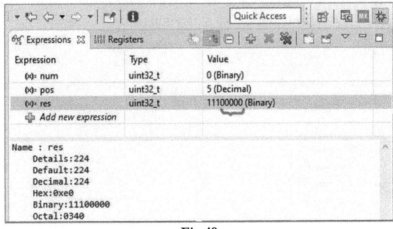

Fig.49

For the parameters

uint32_t num = 0;

```
uint32_t pos = 11;
uint32_t width = 6;
```

the result of operation will be as follows (**Fig.50**).

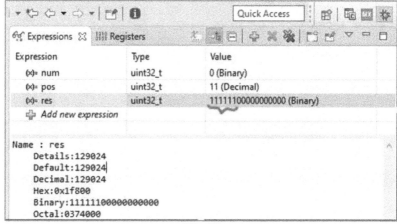

Fig.50

Example 6

The function **rev_hwords()** whose assembly code is shown in **Listing 59** provides fast reverse of the order of the halfwords in a 32-bit word. The function takes 1 parameter in register **r0** that is a 32-bit unsigned integer. The operation is illustrated in the table below.

Before operation	Byte 3	Byte 2	Byte 1	Byte 0
After operation	Byte 1	Byte 0	Byte 3	Byte 2

Listing 59.

```
        .global    rev_hwords
        .text
rev_hwords:
        mov  r1, #16
        ror  r0, r1
        bx   lr
```

To test the function **rev_hwords()**, we need to insert a few lines of code (shown in bold) into the **main()** function (**Listing 60**).

93

Listing 60.

```c
#include "main.h"
extern uint32_t rev_hwords(uint32_t num);

uint32_t num = 139708;
uint32_t res;

/* Private variables -------------------------------------------------------*/
UART_HandleTypeDef huart2;


/* Private function prototypes ---------------------------------------------*/
void SystemClock_Config(void);
static void MX_GPIO_Init(void);
static void MX_USART2_UART_Init(void);

int main(void)
{

/* Reset of all peripherals, Initializes the Flash interface and the Systick. */
HAL_Init();

/* Configure the system clock */
SystemClock_Config();

/* Initialize all configured peripherals */
MX_GPIO_Init();
MX_USART2_UART_Init();

res = rev_hwords(num);
while (1)
{
}
}
}
```

This code converts the value of the variable **num** (=139708) as follows:

Before operation: | 0000 0000 | 0000 0010 | 0010 0001 | 1011 1100 |

After operation: | 0010 0001 | 1011 1100 | 0000 0000 | 0000 0010 |

The result of operation is shown in **Fig.51**.

Fig.51

Example 7

The function **rev_bits()** whose assembly code is shown in **Listing 61** quickly reverses the bits in a 32-bit word. The function takes 1 parameter in the core register **r0** that must be unsigned integer (**uint32_t**). The operation is illustrated in the table below.

Before operation	bit 31	bit 30	▸	bit 1	bit 0
After operation	bit 0	bit 1	→	bit 30	bit 31

Listing 61.

```
        .global    rev_bits
        .text
rev_bits:
        rbit   r0, r0
        bx     lr
```

To test **rev_bits()**, we should insert the a few lines of code (shown in bold) into the **main()** function (**Listing 62**).
Listing 62.

```
#include "main.h"
extern uint32_t rev_bits(uint32_t num);
```

95

```
uint32_t num = 2771983;
uint32_t res;

...

res = rev_bits(num);

...
```

produces the following result (**Fig.52**).

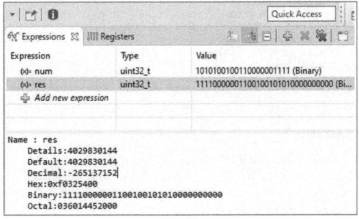

Fig.52

Example 8

The function **read_byte()** whose assembly code is shown in **Listing 63** quickly reads the byte of a 32-bit word. The function takes 2 parameters in the core registers **r0 – r1**. Register **r0** contains a 32-bit unsigned integer and **r1** contains the number of a byte to be retrieved. The function returns the selected byte in register **r0**.

Listing 63.

```
        .global    read_byte
        .text
read_byte:
        mov    r2, #0xff
        mov    r3, #8
        mul    r1, r3
```

```
lsl    r2, r1
and    r0, r2
lsr    r0, r1
bx     lr
```

To test the function **read_byte()**, we need to insert a few lines of code (shown in bold) into the **main()** function (**Listing 64**).

Listing 64.

```
#include "main.h"
extern uint32_t read_byte(uint32_t num, uint32_t pos);

uint32_t num = 72471983;
uint32_t pos = 1;
uint32_t res;

/* Private variables -------------------------------------------------*/
UART_HandleTypeDef huart2;

/* Private function prototypes --------------------------------------*/
void SystemClock_Config(void);
static void MX_GPIO_Init(void);
static void MX_USART2_UART_Init(void);

int main(void)
{

  /* Reset of all peripherals, Initializes the Flash interface and the Systick. */
  HAL_Init();

  /* Configure the system clock */
  SystemClock_Config();

  /* Initialize all configured peripherals */
  MX_GPIO_Init();
  MX_USART2_UART_Init();

  res = read_byte(num, pos);
  while (1)
  {
  }
}
```

The result of operation is shown in **Fig.53**.

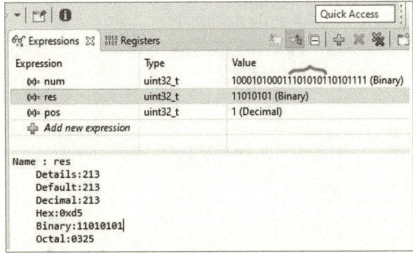

Fig.53

Example 9

The function **test_bit()** whose code is shown in **Listing 65** allows to quickly test a single bit in the 32-bit word using the MCU bit-shift instructions.
The function takes 2 parameters in the core registers **r0** and **r1**. Register **r0** contains the value of integer and **r1** specifies the position of a bit to be checked. The value of a bit is returned in register **r0**.
Listing 65.

```
          .global    test_bit
          .text
test_bit:
          add    r1, r1, #1
          lsr    r0, r1
          bcs    set_1
          eor    r0, r0
          b      exit
set_1:
          mov    r0, #1
exit:
          bx     lr
```

To test the function **test_bit()**, we should insert a few lines of code (shown in bold) into the **main()** function (**Listing 66**).

Listing 66.

```
#include "main.h"
extern uint32_t test_bit(uint32_t num, uint32_t pos);

uint32_t num = 72471980;
uint32_t pos = 10;
uint32_t res;
. . .
int main(void)
{
. . .
 res = test_bit(num, pos);
. . .
}
```

At the given parameters of the function **test_bit()**, the result will look like the following (**Fig.54**).

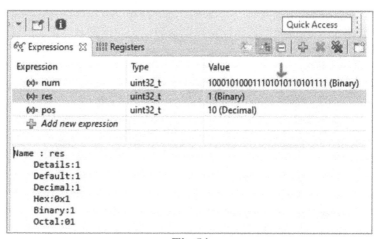

Fig.54

Processing strings

This section illustrates fast operations with character strings using the functions written in Assembly Language.

99

Example 1

In this example, the function **str_cp()** whose assembly source code is shown in **Listing 67** allows to quickly copy a null-terminated string into some memory buffer. The function takes 2 parameters in the core registers **r0 – r1**. Register **r0** contains the address of a source string, **r1** contains the address of a destination memory buffer.

Listing 67.

```
        .global    str_cp
        .text
str_cp:
        ldrb    r2, [r0]
        strb    r2, [r1]
        add     r0, r0, #1
        add     r1, r1, #1
        cmp     r2, #0
        bne     str_cp
        bx      lr
```

In this code, we check if the end of a source string is reached using the instruction

cmp   r2, #0

The iterations continue while the value in **r2** ≠ 0.

To test the function **str_cp()**, we should insert a few lines of code (shown in bold) into the **main()** function (**Listing 68**).

Listing 68.

```
#include "main.h"
extern void str_cp(uint8_t *src, uint8_t *dest);
char src[] = "1234567890";
char dest[32];
```

/* Private variables ---*/
UART_HandleTypeDef huart2;

/* USER CODE BEGIN PV */

100

/* USER CODE END PV */

```
/* Private function prototypes -------------------------------------------*/
void SystemClock_Config(void);
static void MX_GPIO_Init(void);
static void MX_USART2_UART_Init(void);

int main(void)
{

  /* Reset of all peripherals, Initializes the Flash interface and the Systick. */
  HAL_Init();

  /* Configure the system clock */
  SystemClock_Config();

  /* Initialize all configured peripherals */
  MX_GPIO_Init();
  MX_USART2_UART_Init();

  str_cp((uint8_t*)src, (uint8_t*)dest);

  while (1)
  {
  }
}
```

When we start debugging, add the **src** and **dest** variables to the
Expressions window. Before the operation begins, the **src** and **dest** arrays
contain the following values (**Fig.55**).

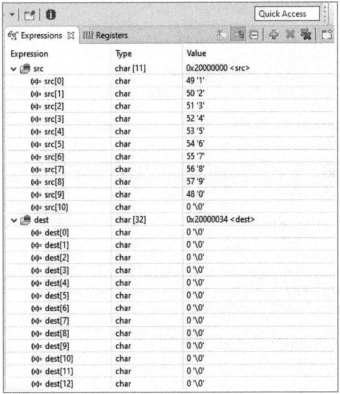

Fig.55

After the operation is complete, the values in the **dest** array change to the following (**Fig.56**).

Expression	Type	Value
∨ 🖥 src	char [11]	0x20000000 <src>
(x)= src[0]	char	49 '1'
(x)= src[1]	char	50 '2'
(x)= src[2]	char	51 '3'
(x)= src[3]	char	52 '4'
(x)= src[4]	char	53 '5'
(x)= src[5]	char	54 '6'
(x)= src[6]	char	55 '7'
(x)= src[7]	char	56 '8'
(x)= src[8]	char	57 '9'
(x)= src[9]	char	48 '0'
(x)= src[10]	char	0 '\0'
∨ 🖥 dest	char [32]	0x20000034 <dest>
(x)= dest[0]	char	49 '1'
(x)= dest[1]	char	50 '2'
(x)= dest[2]	char	51 '3'
(x)= dest[3]	char	52 '4'
(x)= dest[4]	char	53 '5'
(x)= dest[5]	char	54 '6'
(x)= dest[6]	char	55 '7'
(x)= dest[7]	char	56 '8'
(x)= dest[8]	char	57 '9'
(x)= dest[9]	char	48 '0'
(x)= dest[10]	char	0 '\0'

Fig.56

Example 2

To copy only a few elements of a null-terminated string to a destination
buffer, we can modify the source code of the **str_cp()** function from the
previous example.
The source code of a modified version of **str_cp()** is shown in **Listing 69**.
The function takes 3 parameters in registers **r0 – r2**. Register **r0** points to the
address of source string, **r1** points to a destination memory buffer and **r2**
specifies the number of bytes to be copied.

Listing 69.

```
            .global    str_cp
            .text
str_cp:
            cmp    r2, #0
            ble    exit
next:
            ldrb   r3, [r0]
            strb   r3, [r1]
            add    r0, r0, #1
            add    r1, r1, #1
```

103

```
        sub    r2, r2, #1
        cmp    r2, #0
        bne    next
exit:
        bx     lr
```

To test **str_cp()**, we should insert a few lines of code (shown in bold) into the **main()** function (**Listing 70**).

Listing 70.

```
#include "main.h"
extern void str_cp(uint8_t *src, uint8_t *dest, int len);
char src[] = "1234567890";
char dest[32];

/* Private variables --------------------------------------------------------*/
UART_HandleTypeDef huart2;

/* Private function prototypes ----------------------------------------------*/
void SystemClock_Config(void);
static void MX_GPIO_Init(void);
static void MX_USART2_UART_Init(void);

int main(void)
{

  /* Reset of all peripherals, Initializes the Flash interface and the Systick. */
  HAL_Init();

  /* Configure the system clock */
  SystemClock_Config();

  /* Initialize all configured peripherals */
  MX_GPIO_Init();
  MX_USART2_UART_Init();

  str_cp((uint8_t*)src, (uint8_t*)dest, 3);

  while (1)
  {
  }
}
```

The result of the operation is shown in **Fig.57**.

Expression	Type	Value
∨ 🗃 src	char [11]	0x20000000 <src>
(x)= src[0]	char	49 '1'
(x)= src[1]	char	50 '2'
(x)= src[2]	char	51 '3'
(x)= src[3]	char	52 '4'
(x)= src[4]	char	53 '5'
(x)= src[5]	char	54 '6'
(x)= src[6]	char	55 '7'
(x)= src[7]	char	56 '8'
(x)= src[8]	char	57 '9'
(x)= src[9]	char	48 '0'
(x)= src[10]	char	0 '\0'
∨ 🗃 dest	char [32]	0x20000034 <dest>
(x)= dest[0]	char	49 '1'
(x)= dest[1]	char	50 '2'
(x)= dest[2]	char	51 '3'
(x)= dest[3]	char	0 '\0'
(x)= dest[4]	char	0 '\0'

Fig.57

Example 3

To compare N elements of two strings, we can use the function
cmp_strings()) whose source is shown in **Listing 71**. The function takes 3
parameters in registers **r0 – r2**. Register **r0** contains the address of a first
string, **r1** contains the address of a second string and register **r2** specifies the
number of elements to be compared. The function returns 1 in register **r0** if
all selected elements are equal and -1 if some elements are different.

Listing 71.

```
        .global    cmp_strings
        .text
cmp_strings:
        cmp    r2, #0
        ble    exit
next:
        ldrb   r3, [r0]
        ldrb   r4, [r1]
        cmp    r3, r4
        bne    not_equal
        sub    r2, r2, #1
        cmp    r2, #0
```

105

```
            beq     equal
            add     r0, r0, #1
            add     r1, r1, #1
            b       next
not_equal:
            ldr     r0, =-1
            b       exit
equal:
            ldr     r0, =1
exit:
            bx      lr
```

To test the function **cmp_strings()**, we need to insert a few lines of code (shown in bold) into the **main()** function (**Listing 72**).

Listing 72.

```
#include "main.h"
extern int cmp_strings(uint8_t *src, uint8_t *dest, int len);
char src[] = "1234567890";
char dest[] = "1230567890";
int len = 5;
int res;

/* Private variables -----------------------------------------------*/
UART_HandleTypeDef huart2;

/* Private function prototypes -------------------------------------*/
void SystemClock_Config(void);
static void MX_GPIO_Init(void);
static void MX_USART2_UART_Init(void);

int main(void)
{
 /* Reset of all peripherals, Initializes the Flash interface and the Systick. */
  HAL_Init();

 /* Configure the system clock */
  SystemClock_Config();

 /* Initialize all configured peripherals */
  MX_GPIO_Init();
  MX_USART2_UART_Init();
```

```
res = cmp_strings((uint8_t*)src, (uint8_t*)dest, len);

while (1)
  {
  }
}
```

With the given parameters, the result of the operation will be as follows (**Fig.58**).

Expression	Type	Value
∨ src	char [11]	0x20000000 <src>
src[0]	char	49 '1'
src[1]	char	50 '2'
src[2]	char	51 '3'
src[3]	char	52 '4'
src[4]	char	53 '5'
src[5]	char	54 '6'
src[6]	char	55 '7'
src[7]	char	56 '8'
src[8]	char	57 '9'
src[9]	char	48 '0'
src[10]	char	0 '\0'
∨ dest	char [11]	0x2000000c <dest>
dest[0]	char	49 '1'
dest[1]	char	50 '2'
dest[2]	char	51 '3'
dest[3]	char	48 '0'
dest[4]	char	53 '5'
dest[5]	char	54 '6'
dest[6]	char	55 '7'
dest[7]	char	56 '8'
dest[8]	char	57 '9'
dest[9]	char	48 '0'
dest[10]	char	0 '\0'
len	int	5
res	int	-1 (Decimal)

Fig.58

Example 4

The function **cmp_strings1()** whose assembly source code is shown in **Listing 73** performs the comparison of N elements of two strings. The function takes 3 parameters in registers **r0** – **r2**. Register **r0** contains the address of a first string, **r1** contains the address of a second string and register **r2** specifies the number of elements to be compared.

107

When the first pair of elements that don't match is found, the function terminates and returns the index of these elements in register **r0**. If both strings match, the function returns -1.

Listing 73.

```
                .global    cmp_strings1
                .text
cmp_strings1:
                push    {r2}
next:
                ldrb    r3, [r0]
                ldrb    r4, [r1]
                cmp     r3, r4
                bne     not_equal
                sub     r2, r2, #1
                cmp     r2, #0
                beq     equal
                add     r0, r0, #1
                add     r1, r1, #1
                b       next
not_equal:
                pop     {r3}
                sub     r3, r3, r2
                mov     r0, r3
                b       exit
equal:
                pop     {r2}
                ldr     r0, =-1
exit:
                bx      lr
```

To test the function **cmp_strings1()**, we should insert a few lines of code (shown in bold) into the **main()** function (**Listing 74**).

Listing 74.

```
#include "main.h"
extern int cmp_strings1(uint8_t *src, uint8_t *dest, int len);
char src[] = "1234567890";
char dest[] = "1234567890";
int len = 10;
int res;


/* Private variables --------------------------------------------------*/
```

```
UART_HandleTypeDef huart2;

/* Private function prototypes ----------------------------------------*/
void SystemClock_Config(void);
static void MX_GPIO_Init(void);
static void MX_USART2_UART_Init(void);

int main(void)
{
 /* Reset of all peripherals, Initializes the Flash interface and the Systick. */
 HAL_Init();

 /* Configure the system clock */
 SystemClock_Config();

 /* Initialize all configured peripherals */
 MX_GPIO_Init();
 MX_USART2_UART_Init();

 res = cmp_strings1((uint8_t*)src, (uint8_t*)dest, len);

 while (1)
 {
 }
}
```

At the given parameters, the result of operation looks like the following (**Fig.59**).

Expression	Type	Value
∨ 🎯 src	char [11]	0x20000000 <src>
(x)= src[0]	char	49 '1'
(x)= src[1]	char	50 '2'
(x)= src[2]	char	51 '3'
(x)= src[3]	char	52 '4'
(x)= src[4]	char	53 '5'
(x)= src[5]	char	54 '6'
(x)= src[6]	char	55 '7'
(x)= src[7]	char	56 '8'
(x)= src[8]	char	57 '9'
(x)= src[9]	char	48 '0'
(x)= src[10]	char	0 '\0'
∨ 🎯 dest	char [11]	0x2000000c <dest>
(x)= dest[0]	char	49 '1'
(x)= dest[1]	char	50 '2'
(x)= dest[2]	char	51 '3'
(x)= dest[3]	char	52 '4'
(x)= dest[4]	char	53 '5'
(x)= dest[5]	char	54 '6'
(x)= dest[6]	char	55 '7'
(x)= dest[7]	char	48 '0'
(x)= dest[8]	char	57 '9'
(x)= dest[9]	char	48 '0'
(x)= dest[10]	char	0 '\0'
(x)= len	int	10
(x)= res	int	7 (Decimal)

Fig.59

Example 5

The function **cmp_strings2()** whose source code is shown **Listing 75** compares the N elements in two strings and computes the number of matched elements. The function takes 3 parameters in the core registers **r0 – r2**. Register **r0** contains the address of a first string, **r1** contains the address of a second string and register **r2** specifies the number of elements to be compared. The function returns the number of elements that match in register **r0**.

Listing 75.

```
        .global  cmp_strings2
        .text
cmp_strings2:
        mov    r5, #0
next:
        ldrb   r3, [r0]
```

110

```
                ldrb   r4, [r1]
                cmp    r3, r4
                bne    cont
                add    r5, r5, #1
cont:
                sub    r2, r2, #1
                cmp    r2, #0
                beq    exit
                add    r0, r0, #1
                add    r1, r1, #1
                b      next
exit:
                mov    r0, r5
                bx     lr
```

To test the function **cmp_strings2()**, we should insert a few lines of code (shown in bold) into the **main()** function (**Listing 76**).

Listing 76.

```
#include "main.h"
extern int cmp_strings2(uint8_t *src, uint8_t *dest, int len);
char src[] = "1234567890";
char dest[] = "A234D6789S";
int len = 10;
int res;

/* Private variables --------------------------------------------------------*/
UART_HandleTypeDef huart2;

/* Private function prototypes ----------------------------------------------*/
void SystemClock_Config(void);
static void MX_GPIO_Init(void);
static void MX_USART2_UART_Init(void);

int main(void)
{

  /* Reset of all peripherals, Initializes the Flash interface and the Systick. */
  HAL_Init();

  /* Configure the system clock */
  SystemClock_Config();
```

```
/* Initialize all configured peripherals */
MX_GPIO_Init();
MX_USART2_UART_Init();

res = cmp_strings2((uint8_t*)src, (uint8_t*)dest, len);

while (1)
{
}
}
```

With the given parameters of the function **cmp_strings2()**, the result of the operation will look like the following (**Fig.60**).

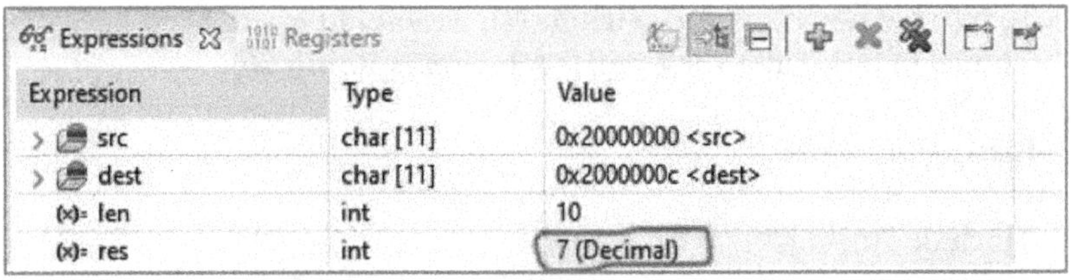

Expression	Type	Value
> 🗐 src	char [11]	0x20000000 <src>
> 🗐 dest	char [11]	0x2000000c <dest>
(x)= len	int	10
(x)= res	int	7 (Decimal)

Fig.60

Example 6

We can modify the previous example so that the function (named **cmp_strings3()**) can count the number of elements that don't match. The assembly source code of this function is shown in **Listing 77**. The function takes 3 parameters in registers **r0 – r2**. Register **r0** contains the address of a first array, **r1** contains the address of a second array and register **r2** specifies the number of elements to be checked. The function returns the number of elements that don't match in register **r0**.

Listing 77.

```
            .global    cmp_strings3
            .text
cmp_strings3:
            mov    r5, #0
next:
            ldrb   r3, [r0]
            ldrb   r4, [r1]
            cmp    r3, r4
```

```
              beq     cont
              add     r5, r5, #1
cont:
              sub     r2, r2, #1
              cmp     r2, #0
              beq     exit
              add     r0, r0, #1
              add     r1, r1, #1
              b       next
exit:
              mov     r0, r5
              bx      lr
```

To test the function **cmp_strings3()**, we should insert a few lines of code (shown in bold) into the **main()** function (**Listing 78**).

Listing 78.

```
#include "main.h"
extern int cmp_strings3(uint8_t *src, uint8_t *dest, int len);
char src[] = "1234567890";
char dest[] = "A234D6h89S";
int len = 10;
int res;

/* Private variables ----------------------------------------------*/
UART_HandleTypeDef huart2;
/* Private function prototypes ------------------------------------*/
void SystemClock_Config(void);
static void MX_GPIO_Init(void);
static void MX_USART2_UART_Init(void);

int main(void)
{

  /* Reset of all peripherals, Initializes the Flash interface and the Systick. */
  HAL_Init();

  /* Configure the system clock */
  SystemClock_Config();

  /* Initialize all configured peripherals */
  MX_GPIO_Init();
  MX_USART2_UART_Init();
```

```
res = cmp_strings3((uint8_t*)src, (uint8_t*)dest, len);

while (1)
  {
  }
}
```

With the given parameters of function **cmp_strings3()**, the result of operation will look like the following (**Fig.61**).

Expression	Type	Value
> src	char [11]	0x20000000 <src>
> dest	char [11]	0x2000000c <dest>
(x)= len	int	10
(x)= res	int	4 (Decimal)

Fig.61

Programming STM32 Cortex-M peripherals: basic concepts

The microcontroller is a heart of each embedded system. Modern microcontrollers are popular for their capabilities to operate with numerous peripheral devices. The Cortex-M microcontrollers contain the rich sets of peripherals for interfacing with the external world (General-Purpose Input-Output (GPIO) ports, Timers, Analog-To-Digital Converters (ADC), Digital-To-Analog Converters (DAC), etc.).

Learning hardware of embedded microcontroller (MCU) may seem difficult enough for software engineers and programmers because of complexity of MCU architecture. and may take a long time. When you start learning embedded microcontroller such as Cortex-M, anyone may feel lost between a heap of information concerning peripherals.
Therefore, may be nice to highlight a few key principles concerning peripheral device operations rather than overloading your brain with numerous and redundant details. These principles are described in this section.

114

Accessing peripheral devices

As we already know, all operations on data (addition, subtraction, multiplication, division, shifting, etc.) in ARM microcontrollers are performed using the MCU core registers **r0 – r12**.

This means that there will be no direct data transfer between two memory locations. Also, no data can be processed at some memory location. If, for example, the program code should check the state of some GPIO pin, it is first needed to load the address of a corresponding GPIO port into some core register, then read the data located at this address into a core register for further analyzing.

To control peripherals such as digital input/output ports/pins (GPIO), timers, analog-to-digital converters, etc. the **memory-mapped** registers are used. Each peripheral device has its own set of unique registers. For example, General-Purpose I/O (GPIO) of STM32 MCU is controlled through the following set of 32-bit registers listed below:

GPIOx_MODER
GPIOx_OTYPER
GPIOx_OSPEEDR
GPIOx_PUPDR
GPIOx_IDR
GPIOx_ODR
GPIOx_BSRR
GPIOx_LCKR
GPIOx_AFRL
GPIOx_AFRH

Each register from this set provides specific functions for an GPIO pin. Using direct access to GPIO registers with the assembly language gives a developer flexible control over GPIO ports and pins and allows to write fast code for I/O operations.

Other peripherals (Timers, ADC, DAC, etc.) are also controlled through their unique sets of memory-mapped registers.

After a microcontroller is powered on or reset, all peripheral devices are put in some predetermined states. A developer must consider these states when writing a code.

Peripheral device interfaces

Basically, reading / writing data from / to peripheral devices are implemented by MCU through interfaces called "busses". This is illustrated in **Fig.62** that represents a very simple hypothetical system with a Cortex-M processor having only two most common types of peripherals – GPIO and Timers.

Cortex-M MCU

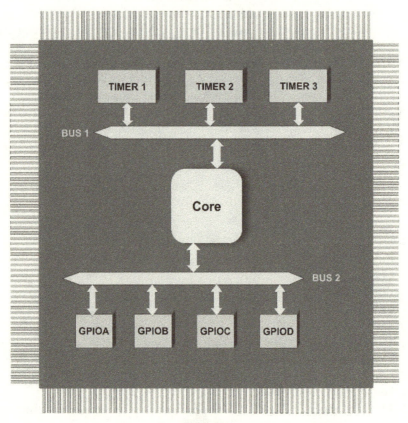

Fig.62

Different peripheral devices may operate with different speed, therefore a Cortex-M microcontroller provides various buses for various devices. In our case, timers **Timer 1 – Timer 3** are controlled through **BUS 1**, while I/O ports **GPIOA – GPIOD** are controlled though **BUS 2**.

Reading and writing data with peripherals

The control of peripheral devices in ARM microcontrollers is provided through a memory-mapped registers. Each peripheral device has its own set of registers whose addresses occupy some dedicated region in memory. The ARM microcontroller when runs some code knows nothing about GPIO, Timers and other devices – it "sees" only the memory region associated with each device.

Let's modify our hypothetical Cortex-M system shown in the block diagram in **Fig.62** so that it can reflect this principle. Now our system looks like the following (**Fig.63**).

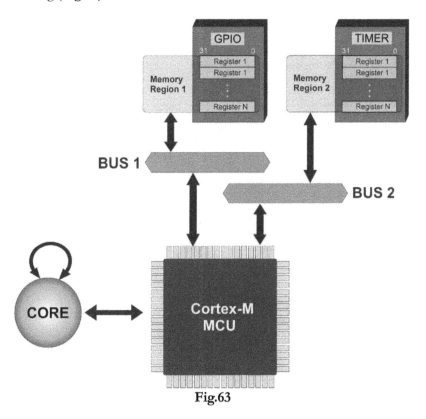

Fig.63

The following excerpt from a datasheet on the STM32L476xx MCU (**Fig.64**) shows the memory regions (boundary addresses) occupied by a few peripheral devices (GPIOs, RNG and ADC).

Bus	Boundary address	Size (bytes)	Peripheral	Peripheral register map
			Table 1. STM32L475xx/476xx/486xx devices memory map and peripheral register boundary addresses	
	0x5006 0800 - 0x5006 0BFF	1 KB	RNG	Section 27.8.4: RNG register map
	0x5006 0400 - 0x5006 07FF	1 KB	Reserved	-
	0x5006 0000 - 0x5006 03FF	1 KB	AES	Section 28.7.18: AES register map
	0x5004 0400 - 0x5005 FFFF	127 KB	Reserved	-
	0x5004 0000 - 0x5004 03FF	1 KB	ADC	Section 18.7.4: ADC register map on page 615
	0x5000 0000 - 0x5003 FFFF	256 KB	OTG_FS	Section 47.15.54: OTG_FS register map
	0x4800 2000 - 0x4FFF FFFF	~127 MB	Reserved	-
	0x4800 1C00 - 0x4800 1FFF	1 KB	GPIOH	Section 8.4.13: GPIO register map
AHB2	0x4800 1800 - 0x4800 1BFF	1 KB	GPIOG	Section 8.4.13: GPIO register map
	0x4800 1400 - 0x4800 17FF	1 KB	GPIOF	Section 8.4.13: GPIO register map
	0x4800 1000 - 0x4800 13FF	1 KB	GPIOE	Section 8.4.13: GPIO register map
	0x4800 0C00 - 0x4800 0FFF	1 KB	GPIOD	Section 8.4.13: GPIO register map
	0x4800 0800 - 0x4800 0BFF	1 KB	GPIOC	Section 8.4.13: GPIO register map
	0x4800 0400 - 0x4800 07FF	1 KB	GPIOB	Section 8.4.13: GPIO register map
	0x4800 0000 - 0x4800 03FF	1 KB	GPIOA	Section 8.4.13: GPIO register map

Fig.64

We can easily reach and control any peripheral device knowing its boundary address. For example, to write data into some output pin of port **GPIOA**, our code should first refer to register **GPIO_ODR** whose address is calculated as a [**base address + offset**]. The base address of **GPIOA** is 0x4800 0000 (**1** in **Fig.64**) and the offset for register **GPIO_ODR** is 0x14. Therefore, the address where to write data will be [0x4800 0000 + 0x10]. For most devices (timers, A/D converters, etc.), we also need to know the speed of data transfer that depends on the bus (**AHB2**, in our example) where a particular device is attached to (**2** in **Fig.64**).

Clocking

All core and peripheral devices of microcontrollers can operate only if they are clocked.
This principle is illustrated by the simplest sequential logic circuit shown in **Fig.65**.

118

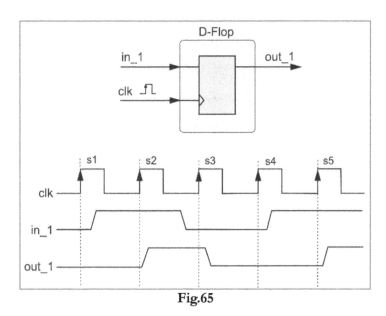

Fig.65

This shows the 1-bit logic element called D-Flop. Such element with various modifications is a fundamental block of any microcontroller/microprocessor system. All registers and memory devices in a microcontroller consist of a various types and numbers of D-Flops. As is illustrated in the timing diagram, signal **in_1** will appear on output **out_1** only if some edge (rising one, in this example) of the clocking signal **clk** arrives at the clock input. The **in_1** signal may be either from a microcontroller (write operation) or some input source such as GPIO or memory (read operation). Again, the output signal **out_1** may be fed to some GPIO, memory or processor. No data will be transferred from input to output while the clock **clk** is inactive.

STM32Fxx microcontrollers have complex clocking systems feeding all core and peripheral devices. It may take some time and efforts to understand how such system is organized. Nevertheless, to start programming it is enough to know a few basic facts about the STM32 MCU clocking systems.

The microcontroller must provide different clocks for different buses for operating core and peripheral device. For STM32 Cortex-M microcontrollers, all these clocks are derived from the system clock (SYSCLK). SYSCLK, in turn, can be configured using either of the following clock sources:
- HSI oscillator clock;
- HSE oscillator clock;

- Main PLL (PLL) clock.

The high-speed external clock signal (HSE) can be generated from two possible clock sources, HSE external crystal/ceramic resonator or HSE external user clock. The HSE has the advantage of producing a very accurate rate on the main clock.
The HSI clock signal is generated from an internal 16 MHz RC oscillator and can be used directly as a system clock, or used as PLL input.
The HSI RC oscillator has the advantage of providing a clock source at low cost (no external components). It also has a faster startup time than the HSE crystal oscillator however, even with calibration the frequency is less accurate than an external crystal oscillator or ceramic resonator.

A main PLL (PLL) clocked by the HSE or HSI oscillator is used to generate the high-speed system clock.
Let's modify our hypothetical system shown in **Fig.63** by introducing the system clock SYSCLK. The modified block diagram of our system will then look like the following (**Fig.66**).

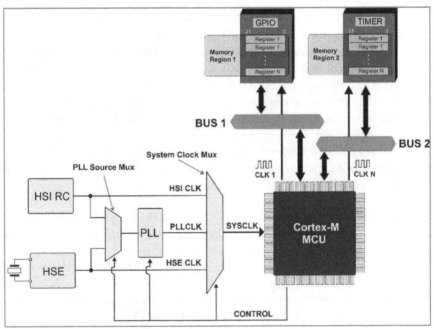

Fig.66

After a system reset, the HSI oscillator is selected as the system clock. When a clock source is used directly or through PLL as the system clock, it is not possible to stop it.

120

Enabling and disabling peripheral devices

Each peripheral device can be stopped or started by disabling/enabling the clock feeding this device. If clocking to the particular devices is disabled, such device is stopped and we aren't capable to read/write the new data from/to the device any more.

Note, however, that the data previously written into a device are kept unchanged even if clocking is disabled (this is illustrated in the timing diagram in **Fig.65**).

The very simplified block diagram (**Fig.67**) illustrates how the peripheral devices can be clocked.

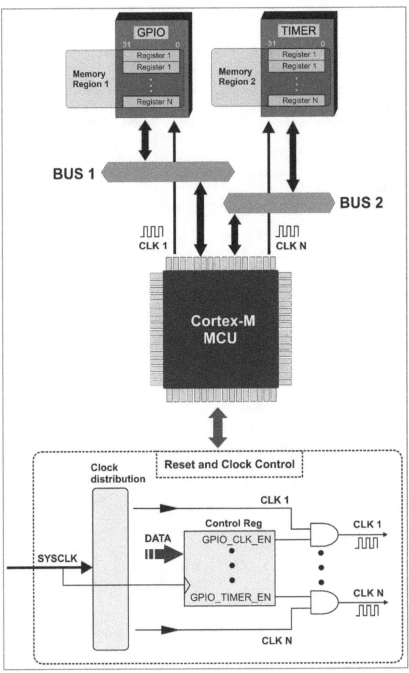

Fig.67

Exceptions and Interrupts

If nothing happens, a microcontroller runs program code instruction by instruction. In real systems, the program flow changes when some exception (event) occurs. There may be various hardware / software sources generating exceptions. The exceptions may be generated by core, floating-point unit (FPU), peripheral devices, etc. When some exception happens, the processor
suspends the current task being executed and executes the fragment of code called the exception handler. After the exception handler terminates, the processor then resumes normal program execution.
As an embedded developer, you will frequently face with exceptions ("interrupts") generated by peripheral devices. Interrupts are usually generated from peripheral or external inputs, timers and in some cases, they can be triggered by software. The exception handlers processing interrupts are also referred to as Interrupt Service Routines (ISR).
Real-time applications usually require to immediately process interrupts that may occur at random time. To provide this, the microcontroller has an interrupt system that should be configured to process interrupts.
Each microcontroller provides processing interrupts through the subsystem whose main part is Nested Vectored Interrupt Controller (NVIC). Now, our demo microcontroller system may look like the following (**Fig.68**).

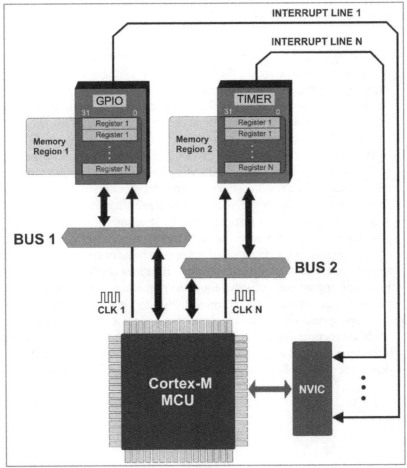

Fig.68

The NVIC and the processor core interface are closely coupled, which enables low latency interrupt processing and efficient processing of late arriving interrupts. All interrupts including the core exceptions are managed by the NVIC.

Pin alternate functions

Each microcontroller has a limited number of pins, while peripherals usually require much more pins than available. For that reason, every pin may be configured to perform a few alternate functions. For example, some GPIO pin can be used as digital output, digital input, PWM output or analog input to A/D converter depending on design.

Below (**Fig.69**) is the excerpt from the datasheet on STM32L4xx microcontrollers where a few alternate functions for GPIO port A are described.

Port		AF0	AF1	AF2	AF3	AF4	AF5	AF6	AF7
		SYS_AF	TIM1/TIM2/TIM5/TIM8/LPTIM1	TIM1/TIM2/TIM3/TIM4/TIM5	TIM8	I2C1/I2C2/I2C3	SPI1/SPI2	SPI3/DFSDM	USART1/USART2/USART3
	PA0	-	TIM2_CH1	TIM5_CH1	TIM8_ETR	-	-	-	USART2_CTS
	PA1	-	TIM2_CH2	TIM5_CH2	-	-	-	-	USART2_RTS_DE
	PA2	-	TIM2_CH3	TIM5_CH3	-	-	-	-	USART2_TX
	PA3	-	TIM2_CH4	TIM5_CH4	-	-	-	-	USART2_RX
	PA4	-	-	-	-		SPI1_NSS	SPI3_NSS	USART2_CK
	PA5	-	TIM2_CH1	TIM2_ETR	TIM8_CH1N	-	SPI1_SCK		-
	PA6	-	TIM1_BKIN	TIM3_CH1	TIM8_BKIN	-	SPI1_MISO		USART3_CTS
Port A	PA7	-	TIM1_CH1N	TIM3_CH2	TIM8_CH1N	-	SPI1_MOSI	-	
	PA8	MCO	TIM1_CH1	-	-	-	-	-	USART1_CK
	PA9	-	TIM1_CH2	-	-	-	-	-	USART1_TX
	PA10	-	TIM1_CH3	-	-	-	-	-	USART1_RX
	PA11	-	TIM1_CH4	TIM1_BKIN2	-	-	-	-	USART1_CTS
	PA12	-	TIM1_ETR	-	-	-	-	-	USART1_RTS_DE
	PA13	JTMS-SWDIO	IR_OUT	-	-	-	-	-	-
	PA14	JTCK-SWCLK	-	-	-	-	-	-	-
	PA15	JTDI	TIM2_CH1	TIM2_ETR	-	-	SPI1_NSS	SPI3_NSS	-

Fig.69

The following two sections illustrate programming two widely used peripheral devices, GPIO and Timers, using the functions written in Assembly Language.

Programming GPIO

This section contains examples of programming digital input /output pins of a microcontroller using an assembly language.

Recall that peripherals of a microcontroller can be reached using the memory-mapped registers. Each peripheral device has its own set of unique registers. General-purpose I/O (GPIO) as any other on-chip peripheral device is controlled through the set of 32-bit registers. Each general-purpose I/O port has the following registers:

- GPIO port mode register (GPIOx_MODER) (x = A..I/J/K);
- GPIO port output type register (GPIOx_OTYPER) (x = A..I/J/K);

- GPIO port output speed register (GPIOx_OSPEEDR) (x = A..I/J/K);
- GPIO port pull-up/pull-down register (GPIOx_PUPDR) (x = A..I/J/K);
- GPIO port input data register (GPIOx_IDR) (x = A..I/J/K);
- GPIO port output data register (GPIOx_ODR) (x = A..I/J/K);
- GPIO port bit set/reset register (GPIOx_BSRR) (x = A..I/J/K);
- GPIO port configuration lock register (GPIOx_LCKR) (x = A..I/J/K);
- GPIO alternate function low register (GPIOx_AFRL) (x = A..I/J/K);
- GPIO alternate function high register (GPIOx_AFRH) (x = A..I/J).

Each register from this set provides specific functions for an GPIO pin. These functions are detailed in the table below.

Register	Function
GPIOx_MODER	Allows to configure the I/O direction mode (input, general purpose output mode, alternate function mode or analog mode)
GPIOx_OTYPER	Allows to configure the output type of the I/O port (output push-pull or output open-drain)
GPIOx_OSPEEDR	Allows to configure the I/O output speed (low, medium, high or very high)
GPIOx_PUPDR	Allows to configure the I/O pull-up or pull-down (no pull-up/pull-down, pull-up, pull-down)
GPIOx_IDR	Input data are brought here
GPIOx_ODR	Output data are written here
GPIOx_BSRR	Allows to perform bitwise write access to the particular bit in register GPIOx_ODR
GPIOx_LCKR	Used to lock the configuration of the port bits
GPIOx_AFRL	Allows to configure alternate I/O function for the low 8 bits
GPIOx_AFRH	Allows to configure alternate I/O function for the high 8 bits

Each I/O port bit is freely programmable; however, the I/O port registers have to be accessed as 32-bit words, half-words or bytes. The purpose of the GPIOx_BSRR register is to allow atomic read/modify accesses to any of the GPIO registers. In this way, there is no risk when an interrupt occurrs between the read and the modify access.

Using direct access to GPIO registers with assembler instructions gives a developer flexible control over GPIO ports and pins and allows to write fast code for I/O operations. In the following sections, we will consider how to perform low-level I/O operations on digital pins.

To illustrate operations, we will use the on-board LED and User button – most STM32 boards contains these peripherals. To control either the on-board LED and/or User button, we must need the pin where these circuits are connected to.

Since we will use NUCLEO-L476RG board to develop examples, we deal with pin PA5 (LED) and PC13 (User Button). Other STM32 boards may use other pins to control LED and User button, therefore you need to adopt source code accordingly.

Example 1

This example illustrates how to set and clear a digital output pin using an assembly code. Our application will toggle the on-board LED (pin **PA5)** every 0.5 s

Launch the STM32CubeIDE and create a new STM32 project (**Fig.70**).

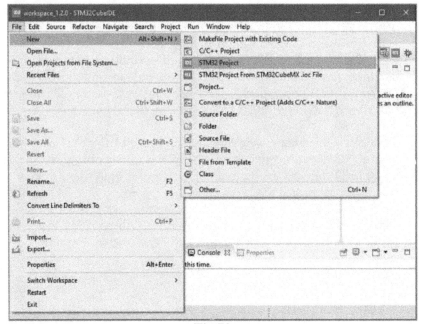

Fig.70

Let the Project Wizard initialize all peripherals with the default settings, then check if pin **PA5** is configured as digital output (**Fig.71**).

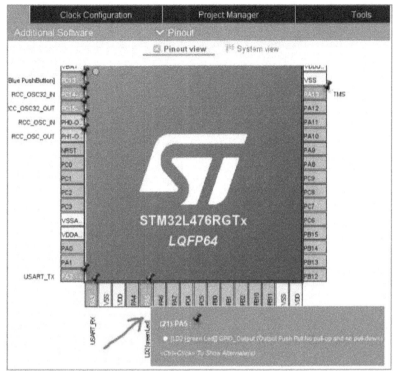

Fig.71

Note that after Code Generator has created the base code for our application, the **main()** function will contain the **MX_GPIO_Init()** function that initializes pin **PA5**. By default, **MX_GPIO_Init()** also initializes User Button (pin **PC13** of GPIO port C) as digital input. This essentially simplifies writing the demo source code for processing digital inputs / outputs.

The source code of **MX_GPIO_Init()** is shown in **Listing 79**.

Listing 79.

```
static void MX_GPIO_Init(void)
{
 GPIO_InitTypeDef GPIO_InitStruct = {0};

 /* GPIO Ports Clock Enable */
 __HAL_RCC_GPIOC_CLK_ENABLE();
 __HAL_RCC_GPIOH_CLK_ENABLE();
 __HAL_RCC_GPIOA_CLK_ENABLE();
 __HAL_RCC_GPIOB_CLK_ENABLE();
```

```
/*Configure GPIO pin Output Level */
HAL_GPIO_WritePin(LD2_GPIO_Port, LD2_Pin,
GPIO_PIN_RESET);

/*Configure GPIO pin : B1_Pin */
GPIO_InitStruct.Pin = B1_Pin;
GPIO_InitStruct.Mode = GPIO_MODE_IT_FALLING;
GPIO_InitStruct.Pull = GPIO_NOPULL;
HAL_GPIO_Init(B1_GPIO_Port, &GPIO_InitStruct);

/*Configure GPIO pin : LD2_Pin */
GPIO_InitStruct.Pin = LD2_Pin;
GPIO_InitStruct.Mode = GPIO_MODE_OUTPUT_PP;
GPIO_InitStruct.Pull = GPIO_NOPULL;
GPIO_InitStruct.Speed = GPIO_SPEED_FREQ_LOW;
HAL_GPIO_Init(LD2_GPIO_Port, &GPIO_InitStruct);
}
```

In this code, B1_Pin corresponds to pin **PC13** (User Button) and LD2_Pin that corresponds to pin **PA5**. The Code Generator will also insert the source code for other GPIO pins that we will configure for our application.

In our example, we introduce two functions, **set_pin** and **clear_pin**, written in Assembly Language. The **set_pin()** function will bring pin **PA5** HIGH (log."1"), while **clear_pin()** will bring **PA5** LOW (log."0").
As usual, we should add both functions (files **set_pin.s** and **clear_pin.s**) to the **\Core\Src** directory of a project.
The source code of the **set_pin()** function is shown in **Listing 80**.

Listing 80.

```
            .global    set_pin
            .text
            gpioa_odr = 0x48000000 + 0x14
set_pin:
            ldr   r0,  =gpioa_odr
            ldr   r1,  [r0]
            mov   r2,  #0x1<<5
            orr   r1,  r1,  r2
            str   r1,  [r0]
            bx    lr
```

Since we have already initialized pin **PA5** as digital output, we can set this pin using the memory-mapped register GPIO_ODR whose address is assigned to **gpioa_odr**. The address of register GPIO_ODR of Port A is loaded into the core register **r0** by the instruction

ldr r0, =gpioa_odr

Then we load the contents of **r0** into register **r1** by the instruction

ldr r1, [r0]

At this point, register **r1** contains the value of all bits of GPIOA. To set a particular pin, the **orr** instruction is used. Then the value of register **r1** is stored back into the memory-mapped register GPIO_ODR.

The source code of **clear_pin()** is shown in **Listing 81**.

Listing 81.

```
        .global    clear_pin
        .text
        gpioa_odr = 0x48000000 + 0x14
clear_pin:
        ldr     r0, =gpioa_odr
        ldr     r1, [r0]
        mov     r2, #0x1<<5
        bic     r1, r1, r2
        str     r1, [r0]
        bx      lr
```

In this code, clearing pin **PA5** (bit 5 of GPIOA) is performed using the instruction

bic r1, r1, r2

To test both **set_pin()** and **clear_pin()** functions, we need to modify the source code of the **main()** function by inserting the following lines (shown in bold) into the **main()** function (**Listing 82**).

Listing 82.

```
#include "main.h"
extern void set_pin(void);
extern void clear_pin(void);
```

. . .

```
/* USER CODE BEGIN WHILE */
while (1)
{
/* USER CODE END WHILE */
set_pin();
HAL_Delay(500);
clear_pin();
HAL_Delay(500);
/* USER CODE BEGIN 3 */
}
/* USER CODE END 3 */
```

. . .

In this code, pin **PA5** is controlled within a **while(1)** loop. In each iteration, **PA5** goes HIGH after **set_pin()** is invoked. This state is kept during 0.5 s (function **HAL_Delay(500)**). Then **PA5** goes LOW after invoking **clear_pin()** and remains in this state during 0.5 s. Then the loop repeats.

To simplify design, we can put the source code of both **set_pin()** and **clear_pin()** in the same file, say, **funcs.s**. As usual, this file should be added to the **\Core\Src** directory of the project. The contents of **funcs.s** will then look like the following (**Listing 83**).

Listing 83.

```
            .global    set_pin, clear_pin
            .text
            gpioa_odr = 0x48000000 + 0x14
set_pin:
            ldr    r0, =gpioa_odr
            ldr    r1, [r0]
            mov    r2, #0x1<<5
            orr    r1, r1, r2
            str    r1, [r0]
            bx     lr
clear_pin:
            ldr    r0, =gpioa_odr
            ldr    r1, [r0]
            movw   r2, #0x1<<5
            bic    r1, r1, r2
            str    r1, [r0]
            bx     lr
```

Example 2

We can also control bits of GPIO using the memory-mapped register GPIO_BSRR. **Note** that using the GPIO_BSRR register allows atomic read/modify accesses to any of the GPIO registers that minimizes the risk of an interrupt occurring between the read and the modify access.
In this case, the source code of **set_pin()** and **clear_pin()** functions will change as is shown **Listing 84**.

Listing 84.

```
        .global   set_pin, clear_pin
        .text
        gpioa_bsrr = 0x48000000 + 0x18

set_pin:
        ldr   r0, =gpioa_bsrr
        ldr   r1, [r0]
        mov   r2, #0x1
        lsl   r2, r2, #5
        orr   r1, r1, r2

        mov   r2, #0x1
        lsl   r2, r2, #21
        bic   r1, r1, r2
        str   r1, [r0]
        bx    lr
clear_pin:
        ldr   r0, =gpioa_bsrr
        ldr   r1, [r0]
        mov   r2, #0x1
        lsl   r2, r2, #5
        bic   r1, r1, r2

        mov   r2, #0x1
        lsl   r2, r2, #21
        orr   r1, r1, r2
        str   r1, [r0]
        bx    lr
```

Example 3

To toggle the GPIO pin **PA5,** we can also use function **toggle_pin()** whose assembly source code is shown in **Listing 85**.

Listing 85.

```
            .global    toggle_pin
            .text
            gpioa_odr = 0x48000000 + 0x14
toggle_pin:
            ldr    r0, =gpioa_odr
            ldr    r1, [r0]
            mov    r2, #0x1<<5
            eor    r1, r1, r2
            str    r1, [r0]
            bx     lr
```

In this code, we use the MCU instruction **eor** to toggle pin.
To test **toggle_pin()**, we should insert a few lines of code (shown in bold) into the **main()** function (**Listing 86**).

Listing 86.

#include "main.h"
extern void toggle_pin(void);
. . .

. . .
while (1)
 {
   /* USER CODE END WHILE */

   toggle_pin();
   HAL_Delay(500);

   /* USER CODE BEGIN 3 */
 }
. . .

In this code, pin **PA5** is toggled in a **while(1)** loop every 0.5 s.

Example 4

Using assembly code, we can set / clear a few GPIO pins in parallel. Let's create a new STM32 project and configure pins **PA6**, **PA7** and **PA8** of port GPIOA as digital outputs (**Fig.72**).

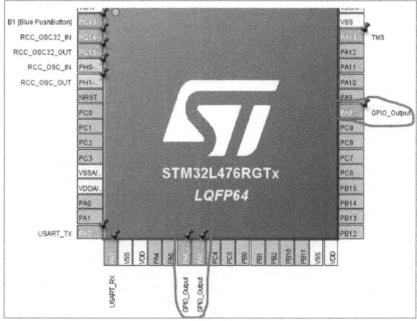

Fig.72

In order to control pins **PA6-PA8**, we will use the function **write_port()** written in the assembly language (**Listing 87**). This code should be placed in file **write_port.s** and saved in the **\Core\Src** directory of the project.

Listing 87.

```
        .global   write_port
        .text
        gpioa_odr = 0x48000000 + 0x14
write_port:
        ldr   r1, =gpioa_odr
        lsl   r0, r0, #6
        str   r0, [r1]
        bx    lr
```

The **write_port()** function takes a single parameter in the core register **r0** that is the value to be written into bits 6-8 of GPIOA (pins **PA6-PA8**). To test the **write_port()** function, we need to insert a few lines of code (shown in bold) into the **main()** function (**Listing 88**).

135

Listing 88.

```
#include "main.h"
extern void write_port(int dat);
int dat = 0;

. . .

while (1)
  {
  /* USER CODE END WHILE */

  write_port(dat);
  if (dat++ > 7) dat = 0;
  HAL_Delay(2000);

  /* USER CODE BEGIN 3 */
  }
. . .
```

In this code, the **dat** variable is used as the parameter of the **write_port()** function. The value to be written to pins **PA6-PA8** changes within the **while(1)** loop every 2 s.

To view the state of the output pins **PA6-PA8**, we should start debugging and open the **SFRs** window (**Fig.73**).

RD | x_{16} x_{10} x_2 | ✂

type filter text

Register	Address	Value
> ▦ OSPEEDR	0x48000008	0xc0000f0
> ▦ PUPDR	0x4800000c	0x64000000
> ▦ IDR	0x48000010	0xc14c
∨ ▦ ODR	0x48000014	0x140
▦ ODR15	[15:1]	0x0
▦ ODR14	[14:1]	0x0
▦ ODR13	[13:1]	0x0
▦ ODR12	[12:1]	0x0
▦ ODR11	[11:1]	0x0
▦ ODR10	[10:1]	0x0
▦ ODR9	[9:1]	0x0
▦ ODR8	[8:1]	0x1
▦ ODR7	[7:1]	0x0
▦ ODR6	[6:1]	0x1
▦ ODR5	[5:1]	0x0
▦ ODR4	[4:1]	0x0
▦ ODR3	[3:1]	0x0
▦ ODR2	[2:1]	0x0
▦ ODR1	[1:1]	0x0
▦ ODR0	[0:1]	0x0

Fig.73

Example 5

One more example illustrates how to stop/resume operations on the GPIO
pin by disabling / enabling I/O port clock. The function **write_pin_en()**
whose source code is shown in **Listing 89** toggles LED (pin **PA5**) until a
counter being incremented every 1 s exceeds 10. When this occurs, **PA5**
"freezes" during 10 s, then the counter is cleared (=0) and the loop repeats.

Listing 89.

```
            .global    write_pin, gpio_enable
            .text
            rcc_ahb2enr = 0x40021000 + 0x4c
            gpioa_odr = 0x48000000 + 0x14
write_pin:
            cmp   r0, #10
            bgt   dis_port
            add   r0, r0, #1
            ldr   r1, =gpioa_odr
```

```
            ldr    r2,  [r1]
            mov    r3,  #0x1<<5
            eor    r2,  r2,  r3
            str    r2,  [r1]
            b      exit
dis_port:
            ldr    r1,  =rcc_ahb2enr
            ldr    r2,  [r1]
            mov    r3,  #1
            bic    r2,  r2,  r3
            str    r2,  [r1]
exit:
            bx     lr
gpio_enable:
            ldr    r1,  =rcc_ahb2enr
            ldr    r2,  [r1]
            mov    r3,  #1
            orr    r2,  r2,  r3
            str    r2,  [r1]
            bx     lr
```

When the function **write_pin()** is entered, the counter that is passed in
register **r0** is checked by instruction

cmp   r0, #10

If **r0** > 10, clocking the port GPIOA will be disabled by clearing bit 0 in the
AHB2 peripheral clock enable register (RCC_AHB2ENR). That is done by
the sequence

```
dis_port:
        ldr    r1, =rcc_ahb2enr
        ldr    r2, [r1]
        mov  r3, #1
        bic    r2, r2, r3
        str    r2, [r1]
```

If **r0** ≤ 10, pin **PA5** (where the LED is attached to) is toggled by the
sequence

```
ldr    r1, =gpioa_odr
ldr    r2, [r1]
mov  r3, #0x1<<5
eor    r2, r2, r3
str    r2, [r1]
```

The counter in register **r0** is incremented by 1 using the instruction

add   r0, r0, #1

This value (**r0**) will then be returned to the **main()** function.
One more function, **gpio_enable()**, whose source code is shown below
simply enables the GPIOA clocking.

```
gpio_enable:
            ldr     r1, =rcc_ahb2enr
            ldr     r2, [r1]
            mov     r3, #1
            orr     r2, r2, r3
            str     r2, [r1]
            bx      lr
```

To test both functions **write_pin()** and **gpio_enable()**, we should insert a
few lines of code (shown in bold) into the **main()** function (**Listing 90**).

Listing 90.

```
#include "main.h"
extern int write_pin(int cnt);
extern void gpio_enable(void);
int cnt = 0;

/* Private variables -------------------------------------------------*/
UART_HandleTypeDef huart2;

/* Private function prototypes ----------------------------------------*/
void SystemClock_Config(void);
static void MX_GPIO_Init(void);
static void MX_USART2_UART_Init(void);

int main(void)
{

/* Reset of all peripherals, Initializes the Flash interface and the Systick. */
HAL_Init();

/* Configure the system clock */
SystemClock_Config();
```

```
/* Initialize all configured peripherals */
MX_GPIO_Init();
MX_USART2_UART_Init();

while (1)
 {
  cnt = write_pin(cnt);
  if (cnt > 10)
  {
   HAL_Delay(10000);
   gpio_enable();
   cnt = 0;
  }
  else HAL_Delay(1000);
 }
}
```

Example 6

This example illustrates how to read the latch of the digital output. This may be useful to exactly know the state of the particular output pin. The function **read_latch()** whose assembly language code is shown in **Listing 91** allows to read the latch of pin **PA5**. The function returns the value in register **r0**.

Listing 91.

```
            .global    read_latch
            .text
            gpioa_odr = 0x48000000 + 0x14
read_latch:
            ldr    r0, =gpioa_odr
            ldr    r0, [r0]
            mov    r1, #5
            lsr    r0, r0, r1
            mov    r1, #0x1
            and    r0, r0, r1
            bx     lr
```

To test the **read_latch()** function, we should insert the a few lines of code (shown in bold) into the **main()** function (**Listing 92**).

Listing 92.

```
#include "main.h"
extern int read_latch();
int state;

/* Private variables ---------------------------------------------*/
UART_HandleTypeDef huart2;

/* Private function prototypes ---------------------------------*/
void SystemClock_Config(void);
static void MX_GPIO_Init(void);
static void MX_USART2_UART_Init(void);

int main(void)
{
 /* Reset of all peripherals, Initializes the Flash interface and the Systick. */
  HAL_Init();

 /* Configure the system clock */
  SystemClock_Config();

 /* Initialize all configured peripherals */
  MX_GPIO_Init();
  MX_USART2_UART_Init();

  while (1)
  {
    HAL_GPIO_TogglePin(GPIOA, GPIO_PIN_5);
    state = read_latch();
    HAL_Delay(2000);
  }
}
```

To view both bit 5 of port A (**PA5**) and value of the variable **state** (**Fig.74**) we should start debugging our application.

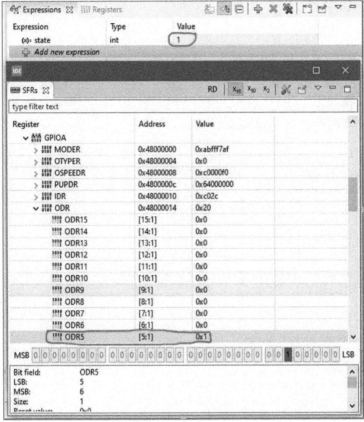

Fig.74

Example 7

It is easy to write a compact code for reading digital inputs using the assembly language. Our application will read the state of pin **13** of port C (GPIOC) of the STM32L476 MCU installed on my Nucleo board. The User button is connected to this pin so we can check how the state of pin **PC13** changes while pressing / releasing this button.
Let's create the new project in STM32CubeIDE with default peripheral device settings and then configure pin **PC13** as digital input as is shown in **Fig.75**.

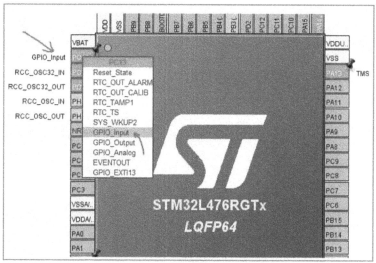

Fig.75

The we write a simple function (named **read_pin()**) to read the state of this pin. The assembly source code of this function e code is shown in **Listing 93**.

Listing 93.

```
        .global    read_pin
        .text
        gpioc_idr - 0x48000800 + 0x10
read_pin:
        ldr    r0, =gpioc_idr
        ldr    r0, [r0]
        lsr    r0, r0, #13
        mov    r1, #1
        and    r0, r0, r1
        bx     lr
```

To test the **read_pin()** function, we can insert a few lines of code (shown in bold) into the **main()** function (**Listing 94**). The code in the **main()** function reads the state of pin **PC13** in a **while()** loop. If pin **PC13** is LOW (User button is pressed), the on-board LED (pin **PA5**) is toggled.

Listing 94.

```
#include "main.h"
extern uint32_t read_pin(void);
```

143

```
/* Private variables -----------------------------------------------------*/
UART_HandleTypeDef huart2;

/* Private function prototypes -------------------------------------------*/
void SystemClock_Config(void);
static void MX_GPIO_Init(void);
static void MX_USART2_UART_Init(void);

int main(void)
{

  /* Reset of all peripherals, Initializes the Flash interface and the Systick. */
  HAL_Init();

  /* Configure the system clock */
  SystemClock_Config();

  /* Initialize all configured peripherals */
  MX_GPIO_Init();
  MX_USART2_UART_Init();

  while (1)
  {
   if (read_pin() != 1L)
   {
    HAL_GPIO_TogglePin(GPIOA, GPIO_PIN_5);
    HAL_Delay(300);
   }
  }
}
```

Example 8

For better performance, we can read the state of digital input using the interrupt assigned to a particular pin as is illustrated in the example below. Our application will drive the on-board LED ON when the interrupt associated with the **PC13** digital input is triggered by the falling edge. Conversely, the LED is driven OFF when the rising edge arrives on input **PC13**.
Before adding the code, we need to configure the interrupt on digital input pin **PC13** (**Fig.76 – Fig.78**).

144

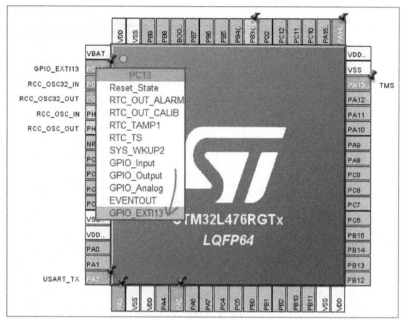

Fig.76

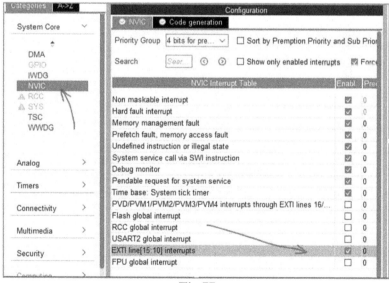

Fig.77

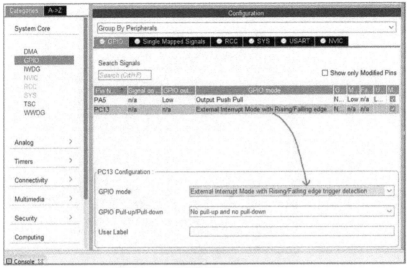

Fig.78

The we need to update the code and modify the source code in file
stm32l4xx_it.c (Listing 95). The inserted lines of code are shown in bold.

Listing 95.

```
#include "main.h"
#include "stm32l4xx_it.h"
extern void write_pin(void);
```

. . .

```
/*******************************************************************/
/* STM32L4xx Peripheral Interrupt Handlers                       */
/* Add here the Interrupt Handlers for the used peripherals.      */
/* For the available peripheral interrupt handler names,          */
/* please refer to the startup file (startup_stm32l4xx.s).        */
/*******************************************************************/

/**
  * @brief This function handles EXTI line[15:10] interrupts.
  */
void EXTI15_10_IRQHandler(void)
{
  /* USER CODE BEGIN EXTI15_10_IRQn 0 */
```

```
/* USER CODE END EXTI15_10_IRQn 0 */
HAL_GPIO_EXTI_IRQHandler(GPIO_PIN_13);
write_pin();
/* USER CODE BEGIN EXTI15_10_IRQn 1 */

/* USER CODE END EXTI15_10_IRQn 1 */
}
```

. . .

Here we add function **write_pin()** to the interrupt handler
EXTI15_10_IRQHandler(). The assembly source code of the **write_pin()**
function is shown in **Listing 96**.

Listing 96.

```
        .global     write_pin
        .text
        gpioc_idr = 0x48000800 + 0x10
        gpioa_odr = 0x48000000 + 0x14
write_pin:
        ldr   r0, =gpioc_idr
        ldr   r0, [r0]
        lsr   r0, r0, #13
        mov   r1, #1
        and   r0, r0, r1

        ldr   r1, =gpioa_odr
        ldr   r2, [r1]
        mov   r3, #0x1<<5
        cmp   r0, #1
        beq   clear_pin
        orr   r2, r2, r3
        b     exit
clear_pin:
        bic   r2, r2, r3
exit:
        str   r2, [r1]
        bx    lr
```

Programming Timers

The STM32 microcontrollers have various types of timers:

- advanced control timers;
- general-purpose timers;
- basic timers;
- low-power timers;
- watchdog timers;
- a SysTick timer.

The advanced-control timer can each be seen as a three-phase PWM multiplexed on 6 channels. They have complementary PWM outputs with programmable inserted deadtimes. These timers can also be seen as complete general-purpose timers. The 4 independent channels can be used for:

- Input capture;
- Output compare;
- PWM generation (edge or center-aligned modes) with full modulation capability (0-100%);
- One-pulse mode output

There are also a few synchronizable general-purpose timers embedded in the STM32 MCUs. Each general-purpose timer can be used to generate PWM outputs, or act as a simple time base. These timers feature 4 independent channels for input capture/output compare, PWM or one-pulse mode output. They can work together, or with the other general-purpose timers via the Timer Link feature for synchronization or event chaining.

The basic timers are mainly used for DAC trigger generation. They can also be used as generic 16-bit timebases.

The STM32 devices may include embed low-power timers. These timers have an independent clock and are running in Stop mode. They are able to wakeup the system from Stop mode.

The SysTick timer is dedicated to real-time operating systems, but could also be used as a standard down counter. It features:

- A 24-bit down counter;
- Autoreload capability;
- Maskable system interrupt generation when the counter reaches 0;
- Programmable clock source.

STM32 Timers can be programmable at low-level using various memory-mapped registers. In our examples, we will use the following registers:

- Control register (TIMx_CR1);
- Counter register (TIMx_CNT);

- Prescaler register (TIMx_PSC);
- Auto-reload register (TIMx_ARR);
- Capture/compare register 1 (TIMx_CCR1);
- Capture/compare register 2 (TIMx_CCR2).

Example 1

This example illustrates programming PWM using Channel 1 of Timer 1 of the STM32L476. The output PWM signal will appear on pin **PA8** of MCU. Initially, we select the base frequency of PWM = 100 Hz and duty cycle (pulse width) = 50%. Then we will change the duty cycle using the function **set_pulse_width()** written in Assembly Language.

Let's create the new project in STM32CubeIDE with default settings for peripheral devices. Since we use Timer 1, we need to select the clock frequency that feeds this timer. To do that, move to the **Clock Configuration** page (**Fig.79**) and select the clock frequency for Timer 1 (this timer is connected to the **APB2** bus). By default, the clock frequency for this bus is set to 80 MHz. In our example, we leave this frequency unchanged and continue configuring Timer 1.

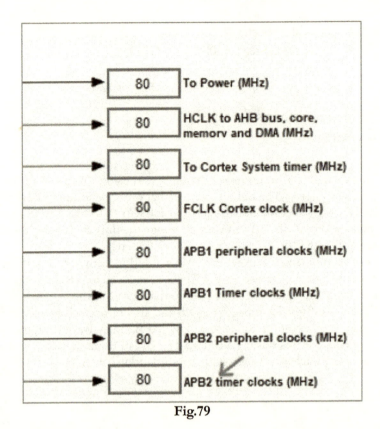

80	To Power (MHz)
80	HCLK to AHB bus, core, memory and DMA (MHz)
80	To Cortex System timer (MHz)
80	FCLK Cortex clock (MHz)
80	APB1 peripheral clocks (MHz)
80	APB1 Timer clocks (MHz)
80	APB2 peripheral clocks (MHz)
80	APB2 timer clocks (MHz)

Fig.79

Then we set the mode of Timer 1. In this example, Timer 1 should generate a PWM signal using Channel 1. The configuration settings for Timer 1 are shown in **Fig.80**.

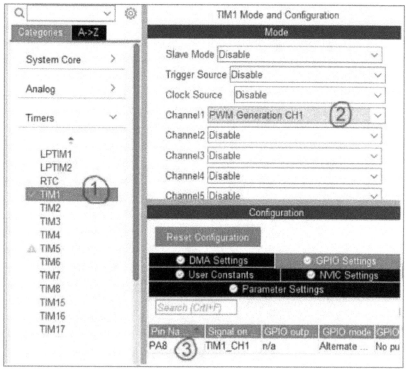

Fig.80

After Timer 1 (TIM1) has been (**1** in **Fig.80**), we select the
PWM Generation CH1 mode (**2** in **Fig.80**). The output signal will then
appear on pin **PA8** of MCU (**3** in **Fig.80**).
These changes will be reflected in the **Pinout View** page as is shown in
Fig.81.

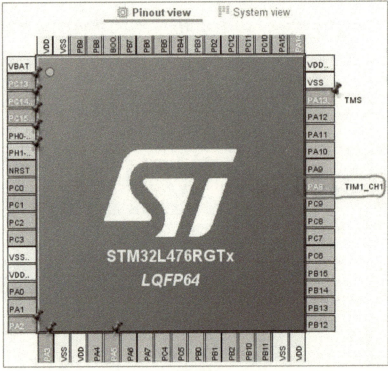

Fig.81

After updating the code by the Code Generator, we will manually modify the source code of function **MX_TIM1_Init()** that provides the initialization of Timer 1. The source code of this function (**Listing 97**) is placed within the **main()** function.

Listing 97.

```
static void MX_TIM1_Init(void)
{

/* USER CODE BEGIN TIM1_Init 0 */

/* USER CODE END TIM1_Init 0 */

TIM_MasterConfigTypeDef sMasterConfig = {0};
TIM_OC_InitTypeDef sConfigOC = {0};
TIM_BreakDeadTimeConfigTypeDef sBreakDeadTimeConfig = {0};

/* USER CODE BEGIN TIM1_Init 1 */
```

```
/* USER CODE END TIM1_Init 1 */
htim1.Instance = TIM1;
htim1.Init.Prescaler = 0;
htim1.Init.CounterMode = TIM_COUNTERMODE_UP;
htim1.Init.Period = 65535;
htim1.Init.ClockDivision = TIM_CLOCKDIVISION_DIV1;
htim1.Init.RepetitionCounter = 0;
htim1.Init.AutoReloadPreload =
         TIM_AUTORELOAD_PRELOAD_DISABLE;
if (HAL_TIM_PWM_Init(&htim1) != HAL_OK)
{
  Error_Handler();
}
sMasterConfig.MasterOutputTrigger = TIM_TRGO_RESET;
sMasterConfig.MasterOutputTrigger2 = TIM_TRGO2_RESET;
sMasterConfig.MasterSlaveMode =
         TIM_MASTERSLAVEMODE_DISABLE;
if (HAL_TIMEx_MasterConfigSynchronization(&htim1,
         &sMasterConfig) != HAL_OK)
{
  Error_Handler();
}
sConfigOC.OCMode = TIM_OCMODE_PWM1;
sConfigOC.Pulse = 0;
sConfigOC.OCPolarity = TIM_OCPOLARITY_HIGH;
sConfigOC.OCNPolarity = TIM_OCNPOLARITY_HIGH;
sConfigOC.OCFastMode = TIM_OCFAST_DISABLE;
sConfigOC.OCIdleState = TIM_OCIDLESTATE_RESET;
sConfigOC.OCNIdleState = TIM_OCNIDLESTATE_RESET;
if (HAL_TIM_PWM_ConfigChannel(&htim1, &sConfigOC,
         TIM_CHANNEL_1) != HAL_OK)
{
  Error_Handler();
}
sBreakDeadTimeConfig.OffStateRunMode = TIM_OSSR_DISABLE;
sBreakDeadTimeConfig.OffStateIDLEMode = TIM_OSSI_DISABLE;
sBreakDeadTimeConfig.LockLevel = TIM_LOCKLEVEL_OFF;
sBreakDeadTimeConfig.DeadTime = 0;
sBreakDeadTimeConfig.BreakState = TIM_BREAK_DISABLE;
sBreakDeadTimeConfig.BreakPolarity =
         TIM_BREAKPOLARITY_HIGH;
sBreakDeadTimeConfig.BreakFilter = 0;
```

```
sBreakDeadTimeConfig.Break2State = TIM_BREAK2_DISABLE;
sBreakDeadTimeConfig.Break2Polarity =
          TIM_BREAK2POLARITY_HIGH;
sBreakDeadTimeConfig.Break2Filter = 0;
sBreakDeadTimeConfig.AutomaticOutput =
          TIM_AUTOMATICOUTPUT_DISABLE;
if (HAL_TIMEx_ConfigBreakDeadTime(&htim1,
          &sBreakDeadTimeConfig) != HAL_OK)
{
  Error_Handler();
}
/* USER CODE BEGIN TIM1_Init 2 */

/* USER CODE END TIM1_Init 2 */
HAL_TIM_MspPostInit(&htim1);

}
```

Since we need to get the base frequency of PWM = 100 Hz, we can do that by replacing the statements

htim1.Init.Prescaler = 0;
...
htim1.Init.Period = 65535;

with the following:

htim1.Init.Prescaler = 8000;
...
htim1.Init.Period = 100;

Since we want to set the initial duty cycle (pulse width) = 50%, we also need to replace the statement

sConfigOC.Pulse = 0;

with the following:

sConfigOC.Pulse = 50;

Timer 1 will not operate until we start it by inserting the following statement (shown in bold) at the end of the function **MX_TIM1_Init()**:

...

```
/* USER CODE END TIM1_Init 2 */
HAL_TIM_MspPostInit(&htim1);
HAL_TIM_PWM_Start(&htim1, TIM_CHANNEL_1);
}
```

While debugging the application, it would be nice to view the signal on pin **PA8**. In my case, I use a logic analyzer that gives me the following picture (**Fig.82**).

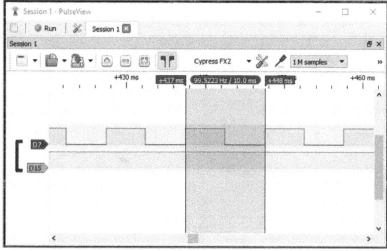

Fig.82

Let's modify our application so that the pulse width of PWM will periodically (say, every 5 s) change. To do that, we will write the function **set_pulse_width()** whose assembly code is shown in **Listing 98**.

Listing 98.

```
                   .global  set_pulse_width
                   .text
                   tim1_ccr1 = 0x40012c00 + 0x34
set_pulse_width:
                   ldr   r1, =tim1_ccr1
                   cmp   r0, #90
                   bgt   exit
                   cmp   r0, #10
                   blt   exit
                   str   r0, [r1]
exit:
                   bx    lr
```

Here tim1_ccr1 defines the address of a Timer capture/compare register 1 (TIM1_CCR1) where the value of a pulse width is held.

Timer1 has the base address 0x40012C00 as is shown in **Fig.83**.

Bus	Boundary address	Size (bytes)	Peripheral	Peripheral register map
				Table 1. STM32L47x/L48x devices memory map and peripheral register boundary addresses(1) (continued)
APB2	0x4001 3000 - 0x4001 33FF	1 KB	SPI1	Section 42.6.8: SPI register map
	0x4001 2C00 - 0x4001 2FFF	1 KB	TIM1	Section 30.4.32: TIM1 register map
	0x4001 2800 - 0x4001 2BFF	1 KB	SDMMC1	Section 45.8.16: SDMMC register map

Fig.83

The timer capture / compare register TIM1_CCR1 has an offset 0x34 (**Fig.84**).

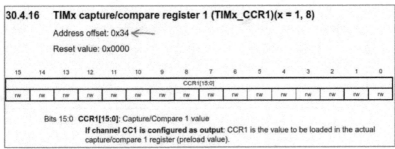

Fig.84

Therefore, the absolute address of TIM1_CCR1 will be calculated as 0x40012C00 + 0x34.

The function **set_pulse_width()** takes a single parameter (the value of a pulse width) in the core register **r0**. The code also checks whether the parameter falls into the range 10 – 90 (the **cmp** instructions).

To test the function **set_pulse_width()**, we need to modify the source code of the **main()** function by adding a few lines of code (shown in bold in **Listing 99**).

Listing 99.

#include "main.h"

```c
extern void set_pulse_width(int pw);

/* Private variables ----------------------------------------------------*/
TIM_HandleTypeDef htim1;

UART_HandleTypeDef huart2;

/* Private function prototypes ------------------------------------------*/
void SystemClock_Config(void);
static void MX_GPIO_Init(void);
static void MX_USART2_UART_Init(void);
static void MX_TIM1_Init(void);

int main(void)
{

  /* Reset of all peripherals, Initializes the Flash interface and the Systick. */
  HAL_Init();

  /* Configure the system clock */
  SystemClock_Config();

  /* Initialize all configured peripherals */
  MX_GPIO_Init();
  MX_USART2_UART_Init();
  MX_TIM1_Init();

  while (1)
  {
  /* USER CODE END WHILE */

    HAL_Delay(5000);
    set_pulse_width(80);
    HAL_Delay(5000);
    set_pulse_width(20);

  /* USER CODE BEGIN 3 */
  }
  /* USER CODE END 3 */
}
```

In the **while()** loop, we set the pulse width either 20 or 80 every 5 s. While the application is running, the PWM signal changes as is shown in the logic analyzer window (**Fig.85**).

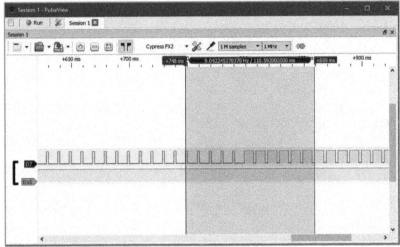

Fig.85

Example 2

One more function named **set_period()** with a source code shown in **Listing 100** allows to change the base frequency of a PWM signal keeping a duty cycle = 50%. The function takes a single parameter (the period of a PWM signal) in the core register **r0**.

Listing 100.

```
        .global    set_period
        .text
        tim1_ccr1 = 0x40012c00 + 0x34
        tim1_arr = 0x40012c00 + 0x2c
set_period:
        cmp    r0, #200
        bgt    exit
        cmp    r0, #100
        blt    exit
        ldr    r1, =tim1_arr
        ldr    r2, =tim1_ccr1
        str    r0, [r1]
        mov    r3, #2
```

158

```
        udiv   r0, r0, r3
        str    r0, [r2]
exit:
        bx     lr
```

With this code, we can set the period of PWM between 10 mS that corresponds to the frequency of 100 Hz) and 20 mS (50 Hz). To do that, we write the desired value into the timer auto-reload register TIM1_ARR whose absolute address is defined as 0x40012C00 + 0x2C. This is done by the instructions

```
ldr   r1, =tim1_arr
. . .
str   r0, [r1]
```

The duty cycle value (pulse width) is set to 50% and written into register TIM1_CCR1 by the instructions

```
ldr     r2, =tim1_ccr1
. . .
mov   r3, #2
udiv   r0, r0, r3
str     r0, [r2]
```

To test the **set_period()** function, we should change the source code of the **main()** function as is shown in **Listing 101** (the inserted lines are shown in bold). With this code, the period (frequency) of a PWM signal changes every 10 s.

Listing 101.

```
#include "main.h"
extern void set_period(int period);

/* Private variables --------------------------------------------------*/
TIM_HandleTypeDef htim1;

UART_HandleTypeDef huart2;

/* Private function prototypes ---------------------------------------*/
void SystemClock_Config(void);
static void MX_GPIO_Init(void);
static void MX_USART2_UART_Init(void);
static void MX_TIM1_Init(void);
```

```
int main(void)
{

    /* Reset of all peripherals, Initializes the Flash interface and the Systick. */
    HAL_Init();

    /* Configure the system clock */
    SystemClock_Config();

    /* Initialize all configured peripherals */
    MX_GPIO_Init();
    MX_USART2_UART_Init();
    MX_TIM1_Init();

    while (1)
    {
    /* USER CODE END WHILE */

    HAL_Delay(10000);
    set_period(200);
    HAL_Delay(10000);
    set_period(100);

    /* USER CODE BEGIN 3 */
    }
    /* USER CODE END 3 */
}
```

The PWM signals captured by a logic analyzer looks like the following (**Fig.86**).

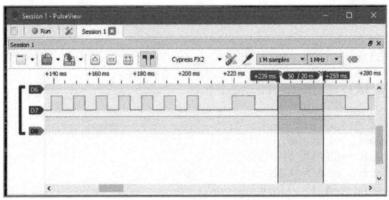

160

Fig.86

Example 3

There may be one more way to adjust the base PWM frequency (period) by configuring a 16-bit timer prescaler (register TIMx_PSC). This case is illustrated below.

Initially, we set the base frequency of PWM signal equal to 1000 Hz and duty cycle equal to 50% by modifying the source of the function **MX_TIM1_Init()**.

To configure a Timer 1 prescaler we use the **set_psc()** function whose assembly source code is shown in **Listing 102**. The function takes a single parameter (a prescaler value) in the core register **r0**.

Listing 102.

```
          .global    set_psc
          .text
          tim1_cr1 = 0x40012c00 + 0x0
          tim1_psc = 0x40012c00 + 0x28
set_psc:
          ldr    r1, =tim1_cr1
          ldr    r2, [r1]
          mov    r3, #0x1
          bic    r2, r3
          str    r2, [r1]

          ldr    r1, =tim1_psc
          str    r0, [r1]

          ldr    r1, =tim1_cr1
          ldr    r2, [r1]
          orr    r2, r3
          str    r2, [r1]

          bx     lr
```

In this code, Timer 1 should be disabled before the new value is written into the Timer 1 prescaler. That is done by clearing bit 0 in the Timer 1 control register 1 (TIM1_CR1) using the sequence

```
ldr    r1, =tim1_cr1
ldr    r2, [r1]
mov    r3, #0x1
bic    r2, r3
str    r2, [r1]
```

Then the following two instructions write the new value held in register r0 into the Timer 1 prescaler:

```
ldr    r1, =tim1_psc
str    r0, [r1]
```

When this is done, Timer 1 is enabled by setting bit 0 in the control register using the sequence

```
ldr   r1, =tim1_cr1
ldr   r2, [r1]
orr   r2, r3
str   r2, [r1
```

To test the **set_psc()** function, we should insert a few lines of code (shown in bold) into the **main()** function (**Listing 103**).

Listing 103.

```
#include "main.h"
extern void set_psc(int psc);

/* Private variables -------------------------------------------------*/
TIM_HandleTypeDef htim1;

UART_HandleTypeDef huart2;

/* Private function prototypes ----------------------------------------*/
void SystemClock_Config(void);
static void MX_GPIO_Init(void);
```

```c
static void MX_USART2_UART_Init(void);
static void MX_TIM1_Init(void);

int main(void)
{

  /* Reset of all peripherals, Initializes the Flash interface and the Systick. */
  HAL_Init();

  /* Configure the system clock */
  SystemClock_Config();

  /* Initialize all configured peripherals */
  MX_GPIO_Init();
  MX_USART2_UART_Init();
  MX_TIM1_Init();

  HAL_Delay(10000);
  while (1)
  {
    set_psc(400);    // = 2000 Hz
    HAL_Delay(1000);
    set_psc(1600);   // = 500 Hz
    HAL_Delay(1000);
  }
}
```

In this code, the frequency of PWM changes from 500 Hz to 2000 Hz every 1 s. The duty cycle remains unchanged as a frequency varies.

Example 4

The functions **en_tim()** and **dis_tim()** whose assembly code is shown in **Listing 104** enable / disable Timer 1 counting respectively.

Listing 104.

```asm
        .global  en_tim, dis_tim
        .text
        tim1_cr1 = 0x40012c00 + 0x0
en_tim:
```

```
        ldr    r0,  =tim1_cr1
        ldr    r1,  [r0]
        mov    r2,  #1
        orr    r1,  r2
        str    r1,  [r0]
        bx     lr
dis_tim:
        ldr    r0,  =tim1_cr1
        ldr    r1,  [r0]
        mov    r2,  #1
        bic    r1,  r2
        str    r1,  [r0]
        bx     lr
```

In this code, we set bit 0 in the Timer 1 control register 1 (TIM1_CR1) to enable counting Timer 1 or clear the same bit to disable counting.

We should save the above source code in file (say, **tim_ctrl.s**) in the **\Core\Src** directory of a project, then modify the source code of the **main()** function by inserting a few lines of code (shown in bold in **Listing 105**) to test both functions **en_tim()** and **dis_tim()**.
The **main()** function code periodically (every 10 s) enables / disables Timer 1.

Listing 105.

```
#include "main.h"
extern void en_tim(void);
extern void dis_tim(void);

/* Private variables ---------------------------------------------------------*/
TIM_HandleTypeDef htim1;

UART_HandleTypeDef huart2;

/* Private function prototypes -----------------------------------------------*/
void SystemClock_Config(void);
static void MX_GPIO_Init(void);
static void MX_USART2_UART_Init(void);
static void MX_TIM1_Init(void);

int main(void)
{
```

```
/* Reset of all peripherals, Initializes the Flash interface and the Systick. */
HAL_Init();

/* Configure the system clock */
SystemClock_Config();

/* Initialize all configured peripherals */
MX_GPIO_Init();
MX_USART2_UART_Init();
MX_TIM1_Init();

while (1)
{
  /* USER CODE END WHILE */

  HAL_Delay(10000);
  dis_tim();
  HAL_Delay(10000);
  en_tim();

  /* USER CODE BEGIN 3 */
}
/* USER CODE END 3 */
}
```

Example 5

This example illustrates use of functions written in Assembly Language within the Interrupt Service Routine (ISR) processing timer interrupts. Here we will use the basic timer TIM6 of STM32L476 MCU (you can use a similar peripheral device available on any STM32 microcontroller).
Our application code will read the state of User button (digital input **PC13**) 10 times/s using the Timer 6 Interrupt. While the button is released (a default state), the on-board LED (pin **PA5**) is blinking. After the button has been pressed, the Timer 6 Interrupt is triggered and ISR is invoked.
The code within ISR disables the Timer 6 interrupt thus causing the LED to stop blinking.

Let's create a new STM32 Project in STM32CubeIDE. Since we use Timer 6 of STM32L476 MCU, we select 80 MHz for clocking. Then we should configure timer TIM6 as described below.
First, we activate TIM6 and enable its interrupt (**Fig.87**).

165

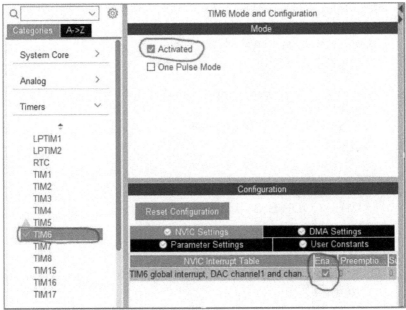

Fig.87

Then we configure pin **PC13** as GPIO Input as is shown in **Fig.88**.

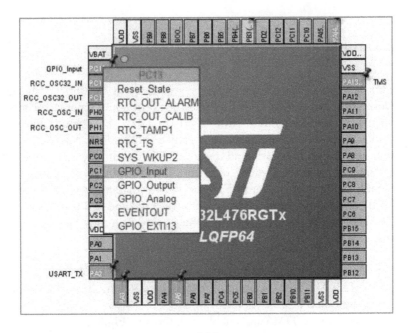

Fig.88

After saving changes and updating the code, we write the assembly language code for the function **inp_detect()** that will perform a job within Timer 6 ISR. The source code of the **inp_detect()** function is shown in **Listing 106**.

Listing 106.

```
                .global    inp_detect
                .text
                gpioc_idr = 0x48000800 + 0x10
                tim6_dier = 0x40001000 + 0x0c
inp_detect:
                ldr    r0, =gpioc_idr
                ldr    r0, [r0]
                lsr    r0, r0, #13
                mov    r1, #1
                and    r0, r0, r1
                cmp    r0, #0
                beq    disable_int
                b      exit
disable_int:
                ldr    r0, =tim6_dier
                ldr    r1, [r0]
                mov    r2, #1
                bic    r1, r2
                str    r1, [r0]
exit:
                bx     lr
```

In this code, pin **PC13** is read and processed by the sequence

```
ldr    r0, =gpioc_idr
ldr    r0, [r0]
lsr    r0, r0, #13
mov    r1, #1
and    r0, r0, r1
```

If the value in register r0 turns out to be 1, nothing happens and functions terminates. If r0 = 0, bit 0 (UIE) in the TIM1 DMA/Interrupt enable register (TIM1_DIER) is cleared thus disabling interrupts forever. That is done by the sequence

disable_int:

```
ldr    r0, =tim6_dier
ldr    r1, [r0]
mov    r2, #1
bic    r1, r2
str    r1, [r0]
```

The on-board LED is then stopped blinking.

The source code of the function should be saved in the **\Core\Src** directory in **inp_detect.s** file.

At the next step we modify the content of the **stm32l4xx_it.c** file where the Interrupt Service Routine codes are placed. We should modify this file by inserting a few lines of code (shown in bold) as is shown in **Listing 107**.

Listing 107.

```
#include "main.h"
#include "stm32l4xx_it.h"
extern uint32_t inp_detect(void);

. . .

/* External variables -------------------------------------------------*/
extern TIM_HandleTypeDef htim6;

/*********************************************************************/
/*    ortex-M4 Processor Interruption and Exception Handlers       */
/*********************************************************************/

. . .

/**
  * @brief This function handles System tick timer.
  */
void SysTick_Handler(void)
{
  /* USER CODE BEGIN SysTick_IRQn 0 */

  /* USER CODE END SysTick_IRQn 0 */
  HAL_IncTick();
  /* USER CODE BEGIN SysTick_IRQn 1 */
```

```
  /* USER CODE END SysTick_IRQn 1 */
}

/******************************************************************/
/* STM32L4xx Peripheral Interrupt Handlers                      */
/* Add here the Interrupt Handlers for the used peripherals.    */
/* For the available peripheral interrupt handler names,        */
/* please refer to the startup file (startup_stm32l4xx.s).      */
/******************************************************************/

/**
  * @brief This function handles TIM6 global interrupt, DAC channel1 and
channel2 underrun error interrupts.
  */
void TIM6_DAC_IRQHandler(void)
{
  /* USER CODE BEGIN TIM6_DAC_IRQn 0 */

  /* USER CODE END TIM6_DAC_IRQn 0 */
  HAL_TIM_IRQHandler(&htim6);
  /* USER CODE BEGIN TIM6_DAC_IRQn 1 */

  if (inp_detect() != 0x0)
      HAL_GPIO_TogglePin(GPIOA, GPIO_PIN_5);

  /* USER CODE END TIM6_DAC_IRQn 1 */
}

  . . .
```

We also need to configure Timer 6 by modifying the source code of the **MX_TIM6_Init()** function as is shown in **Listing 108**. The modified and inserted lines are shown in bold.

Listing 108.

```
static void MX_TIM6_Init(void)
{

  /* USER CODE BEGIN TIM6_Init 0 */

  /* USER CODE END TIM6_Init 0 */
```

```
TIM_MasterConfigTypeDef sMasterConfig = {0};

/* USER CODE BEGIN TIM6_Init 1 */

/* USER CODE END TIM6_Init 1 */
htim6.Instance = TIM6;
htim6.Init.Prescaler = 8000;
htim6.Init.CounterMode = TIM_COUNTERMODE_UP;
htim6.Init.Period = 1000;
htim6.Init.AutoReloadPreload =
        TIM_AUTORELOAD_PRELOAD_DISABLE;
if (HAL_TIM_Base_Init(&htim6) != HAL_OK)
{
  Error_Handler();
}
sMasterConfig.MasterOutputTrigger = TIM_TRGO_RESET;
sMasterConfig.MasterSlaveMode =
        TIM_MASTERSLAVEMODE_DISABLE;
if (HAL_TIMEx_MasterConfigSynchronization(&htim6,
        &sMasterConfig) != HAL_OK)
{
  Error_Handler();
}
/* USER CODE BEGIN TIM6_Init 2 */

/* USER CODE END TIM6_Init 2 */
HAL_TIM_Base_Start_IT(&htim6);
}
```

Index

U

USART2, 14